BASICS
ANIMATION

03   **Drawing for Animation**

Paul Wells
with Joanna Quinn
and Les Mills

Academia
the environment of learning

An AVA Book
Published by AVA Publishing SA
Rue des Fontenailles 16
Case Postale
1000 Lausanne 6
Switzerland
Tel: +41 786 005 109
Email: enquiries@avabooks.ch

Distributed by
Thames & Hudson (ex-North America)
181a High Holborn
London WC1V 7QX
United Kingdom
Tel: +44 20 7845 5000
Fax: +44 20 7845 5055
Email: sales@thameshudson.co.uk
www.thamesandhudson.com

North American Support Office
AVA Publishing
Tel: +1 908 754 6196
Fax: +1 908 668 1172
Email: enquiries@avabooks.ch

English Language Support Office
AVA Publishing (UK) Ltd.
Tel: +44 1903 204 455
Email: enquiries@avabooks.ch

ISBN 2-940373-70-1
ISBN 978-2-940373-70-3

10 9 8 7 6 5 4 3 2 1

Design by Tamasin Cole
www.tamasincole.co.uk

Production by
AVA Book Production Pte. Ltd., Singapore
Tel: +65 6334 8173
Fax: +65 6259 9830
Email: production@avabooks.com.sg

Cover image:
Dreams and Desires: Family Ties
© Joanna Quinn / Beryl Productions International Ltd

Autobiographical storyboard

animator
Richard Reeves

Biography of Richard Reeves

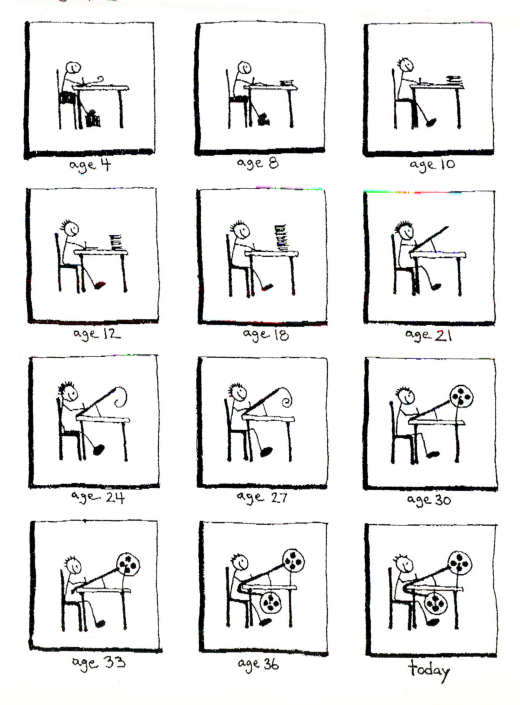

Contents

 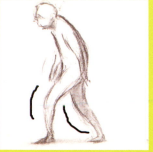 

Introduction

Drawing is a fundamental part of the preparatory stages of virtually all design-led projects. It is the core method by which ideas and concepts may be envisaged and ultimately shared with collaborators, clients and audiences. In whatever form – the doodle, the sketch, the study or the blueprint – the lines and attendant markings, shading and so forth included in a visualisation are the essential representation of information and meaning. Drawing within animation is mark-making in motion, representing the movement trajectories, action paths and character choreographies of animated phenomena. It can operate in myriad ways, from sketchbook work to full frame-by-frame animation, and each performs a necessary and sometimes complex function in communicating particular ideas and emotions.

Many traditional animators combine skilled draughtsmanship with finely honed performance techniques. This combination of advanced drawing methodology and acting has often been seen as the singular and best way in which drawing operates in animation, but it should not be regarded as the only way drawing functions, nor should it be seen as the 'Holy Grail' of achievement in the form.

Much of this view of drawing in animation is inevitably related to the significant achievements of the Disney studio in the 'golden era' between *Steamboat Willie* (1928), featuring Mickey Mouse in his first animated tale, and *Bambi* (1942), the apotheosis of Disney's hyperrealist classical style. Though Disney had recognised the pioneering work of Winsor McCay in *Gertie the Dinosaur*; Otto Mesmer in *Felix the Cat*; and the Fleischer Brothers in creating cartoons that enjoyed their representational freedoms, Disney rejected imagistic anarchy for its own sake and embraced the codes and conventions of performance already established in live-action cinema. In prioritising fully developed character animation and dramatic situation over gratuitous melodramatic riffs and visual gags, Disney's films were able to sustain a long-form narrative.

▼

Halas & Batchelor Studio

John Halas working on drawings for *Animal Farm* (1954), Britain's first full-length feature animation, in which he graphically captures facial gestures performed in a mirror, recreating them in the character of a pig.

It was a consequence of this investment in the animation process itself – a greater commitment to anatomically correct drawing, the stimulus of inspirational art, a recognition of the appeal and format of the adventure narrative in comic books, persuasive character acting, and extensive storyboarding – which enabled the creation of a kind of realism relevant to feature-length storytelling and the Hollywood economy. Furthermore, it privileged a particular requirement for advanced drawing techniques that still characterise 'full' animation in the classical style. In a historical sense, this became especially important because it led to *Snow White and the Seven Dwarfs* (1937), and the acceptance of animation as a bona fide film form as well as a graphic art; a main attraction rather than programme filler.

Disney's achievement has left a long-lasting legacy and remains relevant in the ways that it foregrounds the number of approaches to drawing within the preparation of the final animated film. Disney retrained all his animators in the skills of life drawing, keen that both the human and animal characters should have anatomical verisimilitude. The 'conviction' that Disney believed this gave his characters served to support their narrative function and the anthropomorphic tendencies in his largely animal-based stories. Inspirational drawing enabled artists to experiment with character and environmental design; aesthetics; choreographed postures and gestures; and the narrative and motion potential in still forms.

title
Felix the Cat

animator
Otto Mesmer

Otto Mesmer's drawing for *Felix the Cat* was a subtle combination of persuasive graphic marks and choreography drawn from the pantomimic performances of Charlie Chaplin and other silent cinema comedians.

Drawing for animation

Modernist idioms

Disney's artists were influenced by a myriad of largely European visual sources including the work of JJ Grandville, Doré, Daumier, Kley, Griset and Potter, and ultimately predicated their drawing skills on Western idioms of composition and perspective. Greater degrees of abstraction were found in works such as *Fantasia* (1940), and in the cartoons of the 1950s, which themselves were responding to work from studios such as United Productions of America (UPA), and employing modernist idioms drawn from fine art and graphic design. Disney's classical animation largely remained the same, however, and defined approaches to drawing in animation.

Scholars and practitioners have clearly felt that this is both a benefit and a drawback. On the one hand, this provides a pure vocabulary for drawing in an effective fully animated style, but on the other, it can be a limiting vocabulary for those who cannot technically achieve such drawing, but more importantly for those who would like to work in many other different styles. This book will seek to engage with this perspective and widen the philosophy of drawing for animation, taking in classical animation styling, but suggesting too that there are a number of other approaches and processes in which drawing is central and intrinsically different.

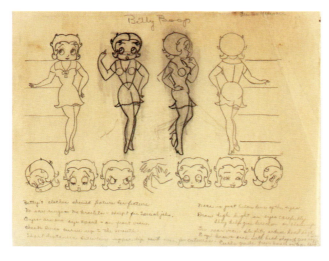

◀

Betty Boop model sheet

animator
Fleischer Brothers

This original model sheet from the Fleischer Brothers' *Betty Boop* cartoons visualises Betty's proportion, posture and implied movement, as well as a number of her facial gestures in the graphic articulacy of her emotional responses. Particular attention is given to the demure, flicking motion of Betty's hand gestures.

One of the most important characteristics of drawing embedded within these approaches and processes is the way in which it facilitates thinking about narrative and encourages the visualisation of ideas and concepts. Further, drawing that suggests narrative events and comic idioms in turn suggests the process by which the movements required to create the phase of action may be choreographed and executed.

Right at the beginning of, and during such processes, the personal sketchbook is often an important tool in engaging with visual experiments, recording ideas, practising particular designs and blocking strategies, trying out perspectives on movement, making observations and creating imaginative contexts to stimulate further material, etc. The sketchbook is in many senses the great liberator from prescriptive thinking or the particular rules, codes and conventions that are often associated with executing full animation, and the long shadow of Disney-style classicism.

Crucially, on whatever terms and conditions the sketchbook or any other preparatory idioms might be used, and for whatever outcomes – character animation through to pure abstracted lines and forms – drawing in animation can facilitate a range of psychological, emotional, physical and material worlds. These will be explored in the following chapters.

◀

title
Man Alive! (1952)

animator
UPA

UPA's work deployed modernist idioms, largely drawn from the work of Saul Steinberg, Raoul Dufy, Georg Olden, Stuart Davis and Ronald Searle, which rescaled, distorted and absented environments, and sought to express mood and outlook through colour, shape and form.

Thinking about drawing

The opening address will encourage readers to see the role and function drawing performs as a creative tool, and a mediator of psychological and emotional expression.

Practice

Having looked at drawing in general, the discussion will begin to look at some of the more typical expectations of drawing for classical animation, but also how this might be varied, and indeed, rejected as a model of drawing in animated film.

Pre-production and production procedures

Drawing plays a role in many aspects of preparing and developing animated narratives and characters, and this is broached in this next aspect of the analysis.

Drawing and narrative

This chapter views how drawing is related to narrative, and concentrates on the particular ways that visual strategies evoke story through concepts, associations and modes of communication.

Drawing and adaptation

The discussion continues by looking at how established drawing styles and contexts are adapted to the animated form.

Drawing characters and concepts

This final aspect of the discussion includes a range of case studies from established artists considering particular approaches to drawing, and how it has been used for specific purposes and effects.

How to get the most out of this book

This book offers an introduction to the various techniques and potentialities of drawing for animation. From the development of an initial idea, communicating concepts with colleagues, and storyboarding individual scenes, characters and stories right through to the final execution drawing is an integral tool in animation research and practice.

Section headings
provide a clear strapline to allow readers to quickly locate areas of interest.

Page numbers
are located on the top right corner of each spread.

There are a variety of methods for generating a script for an animated film. The animator could work with a traditional script, predicated on written descriptors and dialogue or, equally, might work purely through visualisation processes, such as sketching and storyboarding, or even through pure improvisation with particular materials and techniques. Each approach is informed by different intentions and, inevitably, will have different outcomes. What remains significant, however, is the place that drawing has in these scriptwriting approaches, and its common presence as part of virtually every project, whatever the style or approach.

In many ways it was drawing in the first instance that suggested the distinctive ways in which animation could work with symbols and signs as visual short cuts in the representation of human beings, animals, objects and, crucially, ideas and concepts. This offered up the possibility of picturing invisible or seemingly unimaginable things, whether they be complicated theorems or interior psychological, organic, material or mechanical states. Drawing enabled the specific selection of an idea or form to be expressed, and in that allowed for it to be exaggerated, minimalised or transformed altogether.

Once drawings began to move in animation, the additional dimension of time enabled drawing to reveal the past or project towards a future, and to be part of the ways in which animation could seemingly control all aspects of the temporal order or spatial configuration. Drawing – like other materials used in animation – could enable metamorphosis (the seemingly seamless transition from one state or form to another); condensation (the maximum of suggestion in the minimum of imagery); fabrication (the creation of imaginary orders, environments and worlds); and, importantly, offered a vehicle for visualisation that was inherently metaphorical and metaphysical. Another title in this series, *Basics Animation: Scriptwriting*, provides a fuller discussion of this topic.

▶
title
John and Michael
animator
Shira Avni

National Film Board of Canada artist Shira Avni suggests compositional and motion aspects within the frame to instigate a sense of how the animation itself will eventually work. The looseness and suggestiveness of the line itself is highly pertinent in showing aspects of both the physical and spiritual flight in the characters.

Pre-production and production procedures

The inciting idea > **Script** > Storyboard

Captions
provide additional information and directives about how to read the illustration, or historical context.

Chapter navigation
highlights the current unit and lists the previous and following sections.

Drawing for animation

Illustrations
drawings and additional images
appear throughout to provide
insight and information to
support the main text.

Experimentation
42 | 43

Experimentation in both figurative and **abstract** forms is an absolute requirement in drawing and in relation to animation, as it achieves a number of outcomes. First, and most importantly, it is a vital part of developing embryonic thought processes and assists the evolving terms and conditions of invention. Second, it facilitates a call-and-response in the artist as he or she is intuitively 'mark-making' and yet simultaneously going through a process of immediate evaluation and revision while drawing. Third, it enables the process of repetition, selection, refinement and practice to take place as ideas, perceptions and memories are being explored. The drawing is being formed and transformed, translating ideas into marks of interpretation and personal expression.

Experimental drawing is all about not being fixed, nor subject to the rigours of success or failure. It is about the process of trial and error; things emerging from the unplanned, unexpected ideas and concepts forming out of doodling, sketching and placing images in juxtaposition. Ultimately, such drawing is pure opportunity, unfettered by specific needs or goals, and yet may provide the template for all sorts of problem-solving approaches. Experimental drawing can be achieved using different media and tools, and can work within different time frames and contexts. It can also be a vehicle to explore material in a spirit of test and selection, so that a vocabulary of knowledge is built up to choose from in the act of more specific practice. Such work allows and encourages inspiration and the development of a personal style. It will be no surprise that this is essentially at the heart of sketchbook work, and experimental drawing is an extremely beneficial way of expressing and investigating fantasies, anxieties, preoccupations, influences, jokes and emotion.

title
The Wife of Bath
animator
Joanna Quinn
Quinn depicts lustful advances and emotional exchange in *The Wife of Bath*.

Experimental expression
Experimental drawing encourages personal research and investigation in the development of a particular style and mode of expression.

Experimentation is the freest aspect of drawing: in having no rules, conventions or subjects, the artist is free to discover them, and their personal address of them, technically, aesthetically and thematically.

Thinking about drawing

Experimental drawing is all about not being fixed, nor subject to the rigours of success or failure. It is about the process of trial and error; things emerging from the unplanned, unexpected ideas and concepts forming out of doodling, sketching and placing images in juxtaposition.

Paul Wells

Abstract non-linear, non-objective, purely abstract drawing, investigating forms, shapes and colours for their own sake is of considerable importance in animation.

Imitation > Experimentation

Running glossary
provides the definition of
key terms highlighted
within the main text.

Thinking points
seek to summarise,
direct and inform
particular approaches to
practice and analysis.

Introduction > How to get the most out of this book

will either appear
wrapped in cloth or in the
flimsy nightie
we see thru
as I can get
away with.

Anterior

lateral

Two old peop

nervous chattie

She moves with a shuffle and an uneven gait. She
her left hip and uses a stick to walk w

The process of developing animation is just as important as the final creation. Ollie Johnson, one of the leading animators during Disney's 'golden era' (1928–42), suggested that hand-drawn animation is as much about thinking through the process as executing technically well-expressed phases of graphic action, stressing: 'Don't illustrate words or mechanical movements. Illustrate ideas or thoughts, with attitudes and actions,' adding: 'If possible, make definite changes from one attitude to another in timing and expression.' This point is as much about seeing, recalling, proposing performance and delineating concepts as it is about the drawing itself, and implies that drawing for any type of animation is a complex language of expression. We will explore this language by engaging with the possible forms and functions of drawing.

◄

**Hag sketches from
The Wife of Bath**

animator
Joanna Quinn

Though it may be difficult to accept for people outside the arts, all aspects of existence – that which is intrinsically personal, private or taboo, for example – may provide the subject of creative practice, as Joanna Quinn reflects:

'My grandmother was dying when I was working on *The Wife of Bath*. So the hag in it is very much based on my grandma. I know it sounds awful. She was dying, wasting away. She was really old and I was looking at her emaciated body. The human body to me is fascinating, and looking at her, and also doing this film at the same time, I was able then to piece the two together and explore the idea of aging.'

Observational drawing is crucial to animation, even if drawing itself does not figure in the final outcome of a film project. It is not merely concerned with the accurate representation of something that is seen, but a process of recognition and record. Observation is, in essence, the process of learning to see. In 'seeing' the viewer begins to understand the corporeal and material condition of people and their environments and, having 'seen', can process observation in three ways:

Journalistic: an act of personal reportage.

Documentary: an attempt to capture as realistically as possible the thing observed.

Experiential: imbuing the person or object observed with a personalised embrace of the established codes and conventions of drawing in Western art.

Such codes and conventions are often established in the first instance through life drawing. Observational drawing is effectively about challenging what might be known, or is thought to be known, about a person or place by drawing what is actually there 'in the moment'. However, drawing in this way almost inevitably reflects the ways in which the artist has been conditioned to 'see', or taught to conventionally recognise. In observational drawing the hand, eye and mind should be united in expressing what is there. This might be about capturing gesture – a particular action that has significant meaning; recording a posture – a particular way in which a body or form is situated and displaced in relation to its height and weight; or an environment in its present condition – informed by the time and light in which it is seen and employing a scale that takes into account the place from which it is viewed.

Having a drink of water   Castell di fern   20.8.97

A Sleeping Man on the train 21/10/06

Sketchbook materials

animator
Joanna Quinn

Here Joanna Quinn captures the immediacy of the people, animals and figures in order to interrogate anatomy; posture; physical detail; motion; the relationship between weight, size and space; and the sense of the corporeal and material.

▶

Rio Brazil Café Das Artes

animator
Joanna Quinn

A point of view sketch taking into account the forms and movements observed at a café at the **Anima Mundi Festival** in Brazil.

Observational strategies

Observational drawing enables the artist to think carefully about what they are viewing and how they might further scrutinise the often taken for granted aspects of the material world.

In drawing from direct experience, the artist can not merely describe the form, but also analyse it.

In observing the figure or form, the drawing can anticipate the animation of motion and ultimately move beyond what is seen to what might be felt.

Such drawing invests the ordinary and everyday with significance and, in pre-figuring animation, challenges assumptions and orthodoxies about the figure or form.

In looking more closely, the artist offers the observational drawing as a way of seeing the world afresh.

Thinking about drawing

RIO BRAZIL CAFE DAS ARTES 16 Jul

Dick Taylor and Bob Godfrey

animator
Joanna Quinn

A sketch of veteran British animators Richard Taylor and Bob Godfrey in conversation. Quinn captures not merely what characters look like, but their mood, expression and relationships.

Observation > Perception

Anima Mundi Festival an annual animation festival hosted in Rio de Janeiro and São Paulo, Brazil. The festival attracts major audiences for its public vote awards and has expanded its educational and outreach portfolio across the country (www.animamundi.com.br).

Personal perception underpins how we observe, and is bound up with the particular knowledge and visual literacy each person has. Joanna Quinn discusses this idea in relation to her approach in creating the Charmin bear:

'In the Charmin ads we started off by trying to work out what it is that makes a bear a bear. When you draw you take for granted, don't you, what something looks like? You think you know, but soon realise you don't know what it looks like! It's that relearning, going back to the original thing and then starting to take things away from it; trying to find that essence of what makes it what it is. Even if I'm animating an animal I can get somebody to enact a movement and draw it. The thing is that you've got the skeleton there; you can tell where the weight is. With observation from life you've got the truth. You can bend it afterwards if you want to. Even now I still have to have a sheet of definitive bear drawings to refer back to, because he went a bit round at some point and the agency asked, 'Is he changing?' And I said no, and then of course, I looked again at the old drawings and he was changing! So we have a character sheet for reference for the drawings.'

title
Comfy Bed

animator
Joanna Quinn

Joanna Quinn's distinctive drawing style has become the brand identity for Charmin toilet rolls. The softness and ease of the bear drawings imply the same characteristics in the product itself. Here the toilet rolls form a comfortable bed for the bear, whose warmth and charm essentially **anthropomorphise** the product.

title
Beryl

animator
Joanna Quinn

Joanna Quinn's central character, Beryl, challenges conventional representations of middle-aged people. Beryl is vividly alive and takes great pleasure from her physical and material experience. Her body and sexuality – an aspect of identity often denied in those beyond youthful years – are central to her dreams and desires, thus challenging codes and conventions, both in animation and mainstream cinema, about the representation of the female subject.

Anthropomorphise the endowment of human characteristics on animals, objects and environments.

Observation > **Perception** > Memory

The observation of a person or place is inevitably coloured by the way it is perceived. The artist's perception is defined by his or her background, knowledge and context, and the particular way in which the subject is imagined or remembered to be. The artist's recognition of his or her perception – rather than the relative objectivity of observation – of a subject is the first level of abstraction from capturing the subject using the established conventions of realist representation.

At the technical level, for example, this might relate to the perception and depiction of a person or object in relation to a light source, using **endotropic** and **exotropic shadow**. This in itself might determine the space between the material world and the artist; the sense of reality; and the process towards aesthetic interpretation and expression. As in the final animation itself, this may also inform how far the animation wants to be either a reflection of reality; a developmental interpretation of reality, which more readily demonstrates and illustrates the artist's sensibility, technique and approach; or a complete abstraction from reality in which configuration and convention collapse.

In animated films, series or commercials in which a figure or environment recurs, **model sheets** are traditionally used to show the character or figure in a number of poses and positions, or to focus on details in facial expression. This 'fixes' the perception of the character for a number of artists to draw and animate. It is then often the case – particularly with iconic figures such as Mickey Mouse – that more individual or radical artists challenge this 'fixed' perception (and the values, ideological factors and cultural meanings often bound up with it) by re-perceiving such figures on different aesthetic and social terms.

The observation of a person or place is inevitably coloured by the way it is perceived. The artist's perception is defined by his or her background, knowledge and context, and the particular way in which the subject is imagined or remembered to be.

Paul Wells

Endotropic shadow shading that occurs inside and on the form.

Exotropic shadow shading that occurs outside and defines the form.

Model (or character) sheet outlines the size and construction of an animated character's design from a number of viewing perspectives, including detail about the face, hands, feet, etc. This enables a number of animators working across a production to achieve consistency in representation.

The perception of a person or place is part of the marshalling of creative thought and is concerned with the implicit ordering of feelings and ideas. These are themselves influenced by memory, both of learned knowledge and recalled experience.

Model sheet, corrected (1991)

animator
Ward Kimball

Veteran Disney animator Ward Kimball playfully sends up the model sheet, but in doing so signals a range of potential drawing styles from other sources. Here Kimball references Picasso, R Crumb, Fred Moore, Saul Steinberg and Chuck Jones, as well as stylings from genre films, *MAD* magazine and political cartoons, which all reflect different approaches to drawing and expression.

Understanding perception

Perception is often intrinsically related to cognition – literally, sometimes what you see is what you know. Engagement with one's own perception of the world may be a useful tool in the process of expressing it distinctively through drawing.

Perception is also an important aspect of the imaginative process, in the sense that all drawing is predicated on seeking to execute physically what is being created in the mind. A mark of any kind – a doodle through to the extended line – might be the direct expression of a train of thought.

Perception can often foreground a particular insight through the act of drawing, where the immediacy of the mark-making can offer a conscious or sometimes unintentional revision of, or point about, something.

Observation > Perception > Memory

Personal recollection is a major resource to draw from in creating art, and a ready prompt for visual expression. Interestingly, for artists, memory is often related to the ways in which appealing or effective material has already been expressed in other kinds of imagery. Joanna Quinn, like all artists, has significant influences in her formative work, and recognises that she was attracted to a certain degree of realism and authenticity in both the drawing line and the content of the material she favoured: 'I suppose my influences aren't really animation influences. When I was little I used to like *Tintin*, the Hergé comic strip. It was quite realistic, the way it was drawn. It wasn't total fantasy. I didn't really get into comics that were fantasy.... Another influence was Daumier. I love his line. It's terribly loose. If animation were around when he was around, he'd have been an animator, absolutely. And Toulouse-Lautrec and Degas, of course. It just made me realise that they're all based on real life. Putting the line aside, the subject matter always deals with real human beings and grit. The grit of life. And they've all got movement in them. They're obviously static drawings and paintings, but there's so much movement and life in the line. I suppose that's what I was attracted to.'

The Third-Class Carriage (c.1862–64); **La Clowness Looks Around** (c.1886); **Seated Dancer** (c.1881–83)

artist
Honoré Daumier; Henri de Toulouse-Lautrec; Edgar Degas

The influence of Degas, Toulouse-Lautrec and Daumier is pronounced in Joanna Quinn's work, in the sense that each seeks to capture the immediacy of the body's expression 'in the moment'. This involves two key aspects of memory: first, the conscious memory, in engaging with knowledge about art history and technique; and second, sense memory, in embracing the emotional feeling that underpins the expression of motion and the pleasures, stresses and complexities of movement.

Animation itself is the hard copy of psychological memory.

Paul Wells

Memory is an intrinsic factor in the construction of drawing, both in itself and in relation to animated forms. Arguably, animation itself is the hard copy of psychological memory, not only in how the personal context of the animator influences the look of the final creation, but also in using what the experimental animator Len Lye called 'the bodily stuff', ie the meaning at the heart of the expression. Most animators' work is influenced by artworks that they like, and their own drawing and expression is a reflection of the ways they have absorbed this and, further, found their own style. This latter aspect is related to technique, but also to the ways in which drawing and animating enable them to make sense of their own memories. Emotion plays an enduring part in everyone's life and drawing helps to in some way illustrate and define emotion, often capturing profound moments of transition, pleasure, pain and revelation. Animation can elaborate upon the core emotional life of the drawing through exaggeration or understatement, and by advancing its intrinsic narrative, though this might not necessarily be a story.

In animation the trajectories of motion can carry with them meaning and emotive suggestion that prompt symbolic relationships, or associated ideas and insights, which in turn effectively narrativise a visualisation or dramatic situation. Many animations do not have a beginning, a middle and an end, but are visual expressions of memory and, while alluding to sometimes bigger stories and issues, nevertheless function as a narrative embodiment of feeling in its own right.

Where the spirit does not work with the hand, there is no art.

Leonardo da Vinci, 1452–1519

Thinking about drawing

Anatomical studies animators use anatomical studies of people and animals to help them construct realistic motion for a character, based on the extension of limbs, weight proportions, landing strides, etc.

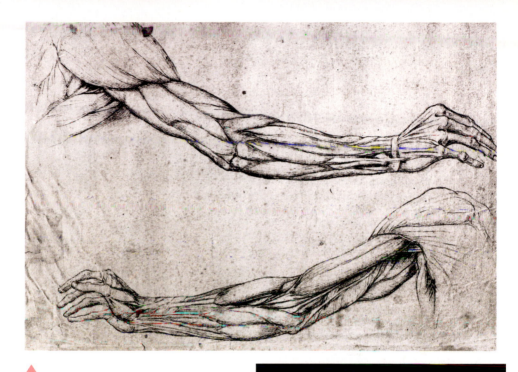

▲

The Muscles of the Shoulder
(c.1510)

artist
Leonardo da Vinci

This **anatomical study**
by Leonardo da Vinci remains as
pertinent in the modern era not
merely for its intrinsic art, but its
approach to life drawing and the
significance of anatomical form
in relation to movement.

Drawing as memory

Drawing is a fundamental and direct
method of recording the sensual
investment in a moment. The drawing then
remains as a catalyst for that memory.

Drawing can become a valuable
aide-memoire to a moment, recording
elements as reminders of things to be
developed and refined in later drawings.

Thinking about, analysing and using
personal memories can be a fundamental
resource for drawing.

Consciously using the memory of what
has been learned about drawing, engaged
with through looking at and analysing the
drawing of others, and improved upon
through practice, is crucial in the
development of repeating animated forms
and movement sequences.

Perception > **Memory** > Interpretation

For an artist working in animation, it is important to apprehend the key ideas and thoughts that underpin an original vision and translate them into moving-image practice. Drawing is fundamental in enabling an idea to find form through visualisation. Although originality is rare, the way material might be interpreted and presented is at the heart of a signature style. Joanna Quinn stresses:

'I think to capture your initial idea on the storyboard is the most important thing. What I normally do is draw the characters randomly and then put a box around them, or draw a box but go outside of it. I try wherever possible not to put any constraints on the initial idea and be as free as I can at that stage, because those first drawings are the most lively ones and they sum up what I'm trying to do. Then I take each storyboard frame, blow it up on the photocopier and make it a size that's nice to work with. After I've captured the movement and energy within the drawing I then look at it critically, often using the mirror to check the perspective. Looking at an image in reverse is like looking at it with a fresh pair of eyes. I make sure that every key drawing is as good as it can be before I move on.'

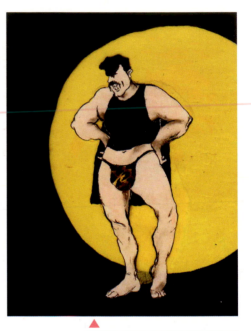

title
Girls Night Out

animator
Joanna Quinn

While the comic strip *Girls Night Out* (1987) (see page 30) has one image of the male stripper, the film can inevitably develop his striptease routine and create a more macho, arrogant performance sequence, which makes Beryl's act of removing his pants – only implied in the comic strip – even more undermining and amusing.

▲

title
Girls Night Out

animator
Joanna Quinn

Quinn's loose and dynamic drawing style richly illustrates Beryl's lustful response to the presence of the male stripper – her eyes and glasses literally pop out. There are echoes here, too, of Tex Avery's influential cartoon 'takes' illustrating overreaction to particular events and circumstances in shorts such as *Bad Luck Blackie*, *King-Size Canary* and *Little Rural Riding Hood*.

Interpretation

Drawing can help with the development of narrative, concepts and the clear expression of a point of view. Each drawing is essentially an interpretation of something.

In creating a story, event, situation or environment, interpretive drawing can show the qualities of materials, the essences of character and a perspective on the person or place.

Interpretive drawing should seek to match style, technique and form to the subject explored.

Interpretive drawing can aid reflection upon, and encourage insight into, a situation or context.

Memory > **Interpretation** > Representation

▲

title
Girls Night Out (comic strip)

animator
Joanna Quinn

Joanna Quinn experiments with visual storytelling in her comic-strip version of *Girls Night Out*, highlighting the key points of the narrative, the shifts in location and character focus, and the idea of a comic punchline. All these factors are helpful in the eventual visualisation and animation of the film.

Interpretation through drawing is a clear indicator of the artist's understanding of the form. In drawing, the artist will inevitably reflect any object through his or her own **gaze**. This reflection is based upon the artist's own vision, experience and desire to represent the object, either to point up something about the form, to consolidate a view, to reinvent the form, or to use the form for a particular symbolic or metaphorical purpose. In animation, it is sometimes useful to recall the variations in interpreting certain **animals**, the characteristics of each representing different intentions on the part of the animator. Felix the Cat is very different from Tom or Fritz; Deputy Dawg is a world away from Scooby-Doo or Gromit; Gertie the Dinosaur is a far cry from those featured in Ray Harryhausen's 3D stop-motion or Steven Spielberg's *Jurassic Park*.

Interpretation, then, is essentially a point of view: a way of understanding something as well as presenting it. From the earliest sketches in an animation project, through to storyboards and model sheets, and the final drawing for a film, the particular view, agenda and visual styling of the artist are embraced. Interpretation is related to aesthetic preoccupations and the desire to make a particular point.

Joanna Quinn constantly engages not only with the act of drawing but the purpose of drawing, and throughout her career has used various methods of researching and addressing her material. Though many animated films relate to works drawn from the history of art, it is the popular forms of illustrated stories, sequential narratives in comic strips and emerging graphic narratives which may be seen to have the most immediate relationship to the animated film.

Winsor McCay's work as an illustrator and comic-strip artist clearly fed into his work as an animator, and popular comic strips such as *The Katzenjammer Kids* and *Krazy Kat* were some of the first to be the subject of animated cartoons. This has become extremely influential in the contemporary era, with many artists working with comic-strip and graphic narrative as well as animation, often adapting one into another and, crucially, using them as tests for narrative development or the construction of comic sequences. Quinn draws upon the construction of the comic strip and the conventions of the American animated **cartoon**, but reconfigures them through her own interpretation.

Gaze a resonant term in both Film Study and Art History that may refer to the artist's interpretive and creative act of seeing, or the audience's way of seeing – scopophilic, invasive, controlling, voyeuristic, etc. Ownership of the gaze and the mode of looking may underpin the creation of politically and ideologically charged representational forms.

Animal representation animal characters combine human and animal traits, which enables deeper characterisation. By not casting and creating human figures, animated films can also circumvent many social, religious and cultural taboos.

Cartoon a contentious term in animation, as it has become singularly associated with the American animated cartoon, thus limiting understanding of the form. The term 'animation' is often preferred because it is more readily associated with a variety of other styles and techniques, as well as production in other nations. Fundamental to the cartoon form is the drawing that underpins it.

Memory > Interpretation > Representation

Representation is often the consequence of interpretation. It has become very important within drawing as artists have sought to redress misrepresentations or under-representations of certain social and cultural groups in dominant media forms. This occurred for Joanna Quinn:

'I went to the **Annecy Film Festival** for the first time in 1987. I saw wonderful films, but saw some bloody awful sexist films too. There were people there who found the films hilarious and I was sitting there thinking I can't believe that in this day and age people are laughing at stuff like this. I couldn't really believe what I was seeing. And then I thought, gosh, you know, I do have a responsibility to make films to try and redress the balance. More recently I think my idea of the men and women thing has shifted somewhat. They're all as rounded and believable as each other now. I was quite angry when I was making those earlier films, quite political. Now I'm over 40 I realise life is not so black and white, and actually quite complex. With our developing project, featuring Beryl, we're having so much fun exploring her husband and other male characters, in a much more rounded way. Before, her husband was a couch potato, but now he's turned into this wonderful person who always wanted to be a vet, but never had the opportunity.'

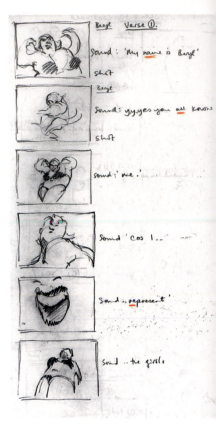

Annecy Film Festival the first and biggest animation festival in the world, bringing together the arts and commercial sectors in a celebration of animation of all styles, techniques and approaches, and informed by historical and contemporary work (www.annecy.org).

Sound: on 'assembly'

Sound: so you think ....

Sound: I'm just a fatty...

Sound: But there's more to me...

Sound: '... than that, see'

Sound: 'and I'll prove it to you now'

▲

title
Body Beautiful

animator
Joanna Quinn

Joanna Quinn's initial storyboards for *Body Beautiful* illustrate her performance in the contest, defiantly championing her own appearance and rejecting the ways women are 'supposed' to look and be, largely in the eyes of men.

In recent years, the work that has informed Film, Media and Cultural Studies in regard to the ideological, political and social readings of creative texts has been properly related to animated film. Animation's distinctive qualities enable artists to create idiosyncratic and highly individual perspectives on the world that are often intrinsically different from mainstream Hollywood film or conventional narratives in short film and broadcast television. These perspectives often take into account the particular address of gender, race, ethnicity, generation and social identity, and challenge some of the stereotypes played out in classical narrative and orthodox storytelling. The versatility of the animated form has helped challenge representational issues. Joanna Quinn in *Girls Night Out* (1987) effectively reversed all the established conventions of looking at women in conventional Hollywood storytelling, by parodying those ideas in gazing at men through the eyes of the middle-aged Beryl as she enjoys denuding a male stripper.

Interpretation > **Representation** > Imitation

▲

title
Body Beautiful

animator
Joanna Quinn

Beryl trains to present her
middle-aged woman's body
as a challenge to the macho,
limited sensibility of Vince,
her sexist tormentor.

Quinn takes this a step further in her film
Body Beautiful (1991) in which Beryl defeats
the sexist Vince, and silences the criticism of
her workmates about her body by training
for and winning a company 'Body Beautiful'
contest. Quinn's drawing is important in
radicalising the perception of the body and
its representational condition. By placing
Beryl's body in flux, Quinn can effectively
draw attention to all the issues by which
people judge others through physical
appearance, sometimes because of their
age and often through the expectations of
social (and artistic) convention.
Representational drawing deliberately plays
with convention and seeks to challenge
expectation by revising, representing, and
re-interrogating the ways in which identity
has been constructed.

Representation and resistance

Representational drawing echoes social
realist or established drawing
conventions, but also challenges them,
either through aesthetic restyling and/or
the particular content of the image.

Representational drawing in this style
acknowledges that ideological and
political conventions have sometimes
become embedded in a particular
drawing idiom, and these are either used
to reinforce such principles, or to
challenge, revise or perhaps undermine
them in some way.

Representational drawing is often a
'norm' in animation because most
animation is challenging the conventions
of realism at one level, and social and
cultural orthodoxy at another.

Interpretation > **Representation** > Imitation

Many artists start out by imitating things they like and admire, or the things they recognise around them. This imitation emerges from an initial reference to real-world figures and contexts, and is often then adapted and developed through processes of reinterpretation and repositioning. Joanna Quinn notes: 'I use photographic reference. If I'm drawing a particular character then I'll go out looking for that character, or try to work out what sort of hair he would have, what sort of clothes he would wear. So when I'm out walking I'll perhaps see someone and think, oh yes, then go back and do a drawing of someone with a certain kind of curly hair or something. So you're piecing it together like a jigsaw.'

▼

Photographic reference materials

animator
Joanna Quinn

Joanna Quinn uses photographic referencing to help her determine the character of the place in which Beryl lives, using the hill-based terraces as a physical challenge for Beryl to encounter as she walks home, and the factory as a model of the modern, foreign-owned and managed workplace. The images also suggest aspects of family, class, economy, history and community.

Inevitably, as well as using particular graphic resources to inform drawn work, other visual and observational aspects are employed. Trying to apprehend a character in drawing often necessitates a degree of imitation. This should not be seen as copying, because the artist is always empowered to use, refine, and rework the initial source; imitation can work in a number of ways, by looking at style, technique, content, structure, etc. Photographic reference might be particularly important, for example, in relation to environments, in the sense that a particular place can evoke a specific mood, create a historical context, a set in which action is going to take place, or become a physical space that can almost play the role of an additional character. Equally, imitation of a known style, character or place – evidenced readily in work by Gerrit van Dijk later in the discussion – can be a clear shortcut to an idea, a time, an autobiographical preoccupation, a signifier of pleasure or pain, for example, and offer an aspect of commonality and shared experience to the audience.

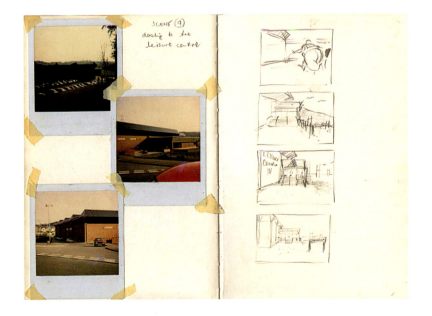

Imitation or imitative drawing can also suggest particular genres. Within animation itself, this has often meant the embrace of, or resistance to, the Disney hyperrealist style. Countries all over the world initially borrowed the Disney aesthetic and industrial model as state of the art, but then drew upon more indigenous stylings to challenge and replace the Disney idiom. In China, for example, the Shanghai Studios used their own calligraphic approaches; in Japan, visual constructions from Hokusai, **Floating World painters** and erotic art; and even in Britain, where portraiture, **satiric caricature** and modern art forms characterised the work. These approaches, in turn, became these nations' own tradition, and were imitated in the works of artists that followed.

title
Britannia (1993);
John Bull's Progress (1793)

animator / artist
Joanna Quinn / James Gillray

In her film *Britannia* Quinn draws upon the tradition of British satiric caricature – here epitomised opposite in the work of James Gillray – to revise the British Bulldog, so much a part of the illustrated representation of Britain in *Punch* and the *Illustrated London News*, and in First World War propaganda films. Quinn imitates but revises this model of caricature to critique Britain's imperial exploitation in its period of Empire.

Imitation as investigation and interrogation

Imitative drawing is not copying but an engagement with an established styling for investigative and interpretive purposes.

Imitative drawing can clearly reference established figures, places, representational idioms as a short cut in signification and communication.

Imitative drawing is sometimes the quickest way to make ideas, thoughts and feelings available to an audience, which may prompt interactive or educational processes.

Thinking about drawing

Imitation or imitative drawing can also suggest particular genres. Within animation itself, this has often meant the embrace of, or resistance to, the Disney hyperrealist style.

Paul Wells

Floating World painters Ukiyo-e art (literally translates as 'pictures of the floating world') originated in shogun-era Tokyo and celebrated urban cultural pleasures. Hokusai, the most well known of the Floating World artists, inflected his work with more of a pastoral idyll.

Satiric caricature political cartooning that offers insight about, and mockery of, political and cultural figures and institutions.

Representation > Imitation > Experimentation

Drawing is such a flexible model of expression that it enables all kinds of approaches and encourages a rich variety of experimentation and risk-taking in the development of work. Joanna Quinn reflects:

'I've learnt over the years to be confident with my drawing. When I start a drawing I know what I intend to draw but I let the line take me in other directions and create forms that I hadn't thought of, especially with the human figure. I love finding different ways to bend the head back or twist the torso just by using line to feel the form. Suddenly I'll see something dynamic and decide to strengthen the line a bit. This is why my drawings have so many lines on them, and why I don't like rubbing them out. It shows my exploration of line, my enjoyment of mark-making. I often have the sensation of not being in control of my hand, that some other force is guiding me, which is probably a common sensation for artists who are totally at ease with a particular medium. My drawings are very loose and yet very considered, and this is why I'm so suited to animation, because animation is all about loads of drawings, lots of problem-solving.'

▶

**Knight riding horse in
The Wife of Bath**

animator
Joanna Quinn

Quinn develops her sense of motion in her depiction of a horse at an unusual angle.

Thinking about drawing

Experimentation in both figurative and **abstract** forms is an absolute requirement in drawing and in relation to animation, as it achieves a number of outcomes. First, and most importantly, it is a vital part of developing embryonic thought processes and assists the evolving terms and conditions of invention. Second, it facilitates a call-and-response in the artist as he or she is intuitively 'mark-making' and yet simultaneously going through a process of immediate evaluation and revision while drawing. Third, it enables the process of repetition, selection, refinement and practice to take place as ideas, perceptions and memories are being explored. The drawing is being formed and transformed, translating ideas into marks of interpretation and personal expression.

Experimental drawing is all about not being fixed, nor subject to the rigours of success or failure. It is about the process of trial and error; things emerging from the unplanned, unexpected ideas and concepts forming out of doodling, sketching and placing images in juxtaposition. Ultimately, such drawing is pure opportunity, unfettered by specific needs or goals, and yet may provide the template for all sorts of problem-solving approaches. Experimental drawing can be achieved using different media and tools, and can work within different time frames and contexts. It can also be a vehicle to explore material in a spirit of test and selection, so that a vocabulary of knowledge is built up to choose from in the act of more specific practice. Such work allows and encourages inspiration and the development of a personal style. It will be no surprise that this is essentially at the heart of sketchbook work, and experimental drawing is an extremely beneficial way of expressing and investigating fantasies, anxieties, preoccupations, influences, jokes and emotion.

> Experimental drawing is all about not being fixed, nor subject to the rigours of success or failure. It is about the process of trial and error; things emerging from the unplanned, unexpected ideas and concepts forming out of doodling, sketching and placing images in juxtaposition.

Paul Wells

Thinking about drawing

Abstract non-linear, non-objective, purely abstract drawing, investigating forms, shapes and colours for their own sake is of considerable importance in animation.

▲

title
The Wife of Bath

animator
Joanna Quinn

Quinn depicts lustful advances
and emotional exchange in *The
Wife of Bath*.

Experimental expression

Experimental drawing
encourages personal
research and investigation
in the development of a
particular style and mode
of expression.

Experimentation is the
freest aspect of drawing: in
having no rules,
conventions or subjects,
the artist is free to discover
them, and their personal
address of them,
technically, aesthetically
and thematically.

Imitation > Experimentation

Practice technique is intrinsic to the way in which an object might be most appropriately visualised. Working in 2D allows the maximum degree of flexibility in the conception of the material, from complete abstraction right through to quasi-realistic configuration of the body and the environment. As has been previously stressed, however, these approaches can operate as a model of pre-visualisation for other methods and developments.

It should be noted, too, that drawing in this sense remains a suggestive and potentially symbolic medium, perhaps using as little as one line to represent something, right through to a confluence of lines in the construction of a particular form. In the context of this discussion, practice also becomes a translation and adaptation of all the psychological and technical engagements noted in the previous chapter.

The template for classical animation was set by Disney during its 'golden era', which established all the techniques for fully rendered 2D animated forms that survive into the present day. Though some have argued that '2D is dead' with the impact of 3D CGI as the dominant language of feature-length animation, it is clear that 2D animation in long and short form will always have a future, and drawing will always underpin the production of a high percentage of approaches to animation.

title
The Wife of Bath

animator
Joanna Quinn

Thinking about drawing > **Practice** > Pre-production and production procedures

Composition and perspective

The emphasis on observation in drawing for animation cannot be over-stressed in the sense that it is important to draw from life, and not from an imagination that would have been already colonised by established image forms. This inevitably leads on to more effective staging of action in which characterisation is achieved through indicators within the visual form: it remains absolutely fundamental that animation dramatises predominantly through its movement rather than its dialogue. The animator must essentially 'perform' through the act of drawing, which in itself must reveal the motives and consequences of the character, shape, line or form in motion. It is this, of course, which led to the development of the basic animation principles (see glossary below).

However, such principles, while remaining crucial to a successful outcome, must also not inhibit the creative expression in working fast and loose, and re-working drawings.

Whiskas advertisement

artist
Joanna Quinn

The first image shows a high degree of **anticipation** as it properly signals the nature of the intended leap. The image of the leap itself shows **action and reaction** by the two cats, and the last image is a clear signifier of the **weight and speed** of a well-fed cat.

Anticipation a model of signifying the movement that is to follow. Before moving in one direction, a figure or object moves back in the opposite direction, effectively pre-figuring the move and offering it greater clarity and emphasis.

Action and reaction most action in animation is in some way caricatured or exaggerated as a clear 'event' which prompts a reaction. Primary action normally consists of forward movement played out through the whole of the body, while secondary action is generally the effect on specific parts of the body or on other figures and objects in the environment, which can often necessitate an equal and opposite reaction.

Weight and speed weight dictates speed: larger characters tend to move more slowly, and their posture is more affected by their weight, while shorter and/or thinner characters tend to move more quickly.

Learning to draw

Joanna Quinn's approach to learning to draw is outlined below:

'Very young children draw from their imagination, but by the age eight or nine they have a sophisticated knowledge of the physics of the world around them and they draw from facts. They use symbols to represent objects; for example, a man with a crown on his head is a king. At this stage the two distinct sides of the brain come into play: the left-hand side becomes associated with logic and correctness and the right-hand side with creativity.

'Then the battle begins: logic interferes with creativity, and it is often the case that potential artists become over-critical of personal creativity. This is usually when people stop developing their creative side, and are socialised into viewing creativity and art as the domain of specialists. Consider the drawing of a retired business professional and it will look remarkably similar to the drawing of an eight year old.'

Early drawing styles

In the first images, six-year-old Lola Wells draws the doll with special emphasis on the colour and flowers, while in the second, the Christmas card focuses attention on the tree branches rather than the robin. This reflects a particular perception and preference in recording the image that tempers realism with the authorial.

Perspective is a good example of the conflict between the left- and right-hand side of the brain and why so many people are bad at representing perspective. Draw a table in perspective and the legs furthest away will be a bit shorter, but the logical side of the brain (the left) will try to prevent you from drawing that because it knows that table legs need to be the same length in order for the table to work. This is why humankind has to learn how to draw. It is important to let the right-hand side dominate the left, which means seeing things as three-dimensional shapes and drawing from life, not from symbols.

For example, in the drawing of a life model it is essential to properly look at the body as a three-dimensional form without associations or preconceptions. The idea of what a person is imagined to be, or should look like, should be resisted in order to avoid assumptions such as 'the arms are too short' or 'the legs are too long'. It is absolutely vital to look at a model as a shape and not as a person, and to therefore avoid value judgements and preconceived ideas about whether your drawing looks right or wrong. Life drawing's concentration on what has been termed '**negative space**' points to its crucial place in the development of an animator.

Body proportions

artist
Peter Parr

These life drawings use light and shade, and positive and negative space, to define bodily shape and posture. The contours of the body are defined through colour conventions. Both images consider the proportions of the body in relation to the angle and position of the figure.

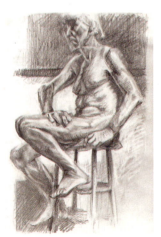

Negative space the area of an image which is not occupied by a definitive shape or form, but which gives meaning to the foregrounded figure. This might be the background, but is more often shadow.

Joanna Quinn's 30-minute life drawing

'To help measure the distances between internal bends and shapes I have labelled them A to H and coloured in the negative space wherever possible, so the surrounding outlines are drawn in as lines defining the internal pattern rather than representing the figure. This helps to see the form as an abstract shape rather than a figure, which is crucial when drawing a foreshortened figure as the left-hand side of the brain goes into meltdown!

'I've also drawn in some imaginary lines that indicate how I measure. For instance, line D measures the length of the body. DA is the top of the head and DC is lined up with the end of the toes. Halfway is DB, so I will draw this area of the leg in. I can now use this point to measure across the body to CC and BC. Everything is cross-referenced and measured against each other – this stops you making left-hand brain judgements of where you think bits should be!'

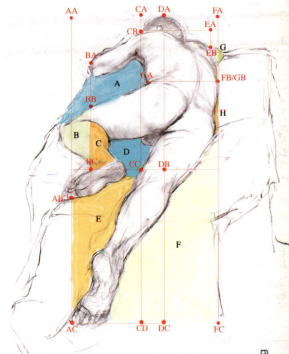

The emphasis on observation in drawing for animation cannot be over-stressed in the sense that it is important to draw from life, and not from an imagination that would have been already colonised by established image forms.

Joanna Quinn

Joanna Quinn's approach to animating human movement

'The golden rule is: when drawing a character doing an action it is imperative to make sure the action is studied before doing the animation, and not after, when you've filmed it and are looking at the movement on the line-tester. Get a model or use a mirror and follow these rules:

▶ Before putting pencil to paper, ask the model to continuously repeat the movement and look at the complete action over and over, attempting to follow the pathway of individual parts of the body, ie the head, each arm, leg, hand and foot, the hips and shoulders. When you think you have a fairly good understanding of the movement, work out where you think the key positions are, ie the points at which the model has changed direction. Once you think you know where the key positions are ask the model to stop at these positions mid-movement and freeze the pose long enough for you to do quick drawings.

▶ It is important to do these drawings quickly as the mind will only search for important information when given a time limit. Think about and discuss, if you can, the function of intuition in recording the movement. Using soft pencil rather than pen, and sketching on big sheets of paper help to speed up the drawing process. Think also about writing notes to accompany the drawings.

▶ Once the **key frames** are drawn have a look at the sheet and check that all the drawings make sense. Can you trace the pathways? Is the positioning of the feet clear? If there is a step, is it clearly shown? Ask the model to do the action again and check that your drawings and notes contain all the necessary information.

▶ Place an imaginary central line on the figure, and look for weight distribution and balance around this line.

▶ Draw the pathway of the moving form – this effectively functions as a line of action within the figure.

▶ Take careful note of the position of feet; this is important in the perception of balance and posture, and helps to identify the key positions the body has moved through. Sometimes in a movement, the feet actually remain static, but facilitate the power by which the move is executed.

▶ Constantly check that for each key pose identified there is a strong engagement with weight distribution, the balance of the body, and a clear recognition of the relationship between shoulders and hips, and the head. Very often the hips work in opposition to the shoulders.

▶ Use heavier lines to show where the weight is.

▶ Once the key frames are done get the model to run through the action again and time it. If it is two seconds and there are five key drawings then you know (very roughly) that there are five drawings in-between each drawing (working on two frames per drawing). This is the basic timing but it is a good starting point'.

Morris Dancers

artist
Peter Parr

Peter Parr captures the ritualistic nature of the movement in the folk idioms of morris dancers. The lines are used not to construct a body, but a figure in motion. This is an impressionist expression of the action, as it is the motion that has been detailed as well as the physical presence and identity of the figure.

Key frame poses the start and end points, plus other significant points of structural change, of a choreographed motion, which must then be 'in-betweened' to create a fully animated sequence.

Initial studies using a model (see previous page) enable the animator to move forward quickly: the studies can be redrawn on to punched paper and become the key positions. The animator can then work directly from the studies and the moving image reference material that has been recorded. The in-between drawings can be done in the normal fashion using a light box and the animator's imagination. It is still important, though, that drawing remains loose and quick. The process effectively becomes one of moving from key pose to key pose, keeping the feet anchored to the floor unless they deliberately step or turn.

In traditional approaches to drawn animation, these key poses, and the drawings that are essentially the 'in-betweens', may be examined by flicking the paper or using a line-tester to see if the animation produces a persuasively smooth movement. The line-tester is great for checking the overall timing and to identify where a pause or greater speed is required. Most line-testers enable you to adjust the amount of time each drawing is on the screen and then work out how many more drawings are needed or which ones should be binned!

The sequence of drawings should be reworked over and over until complete – this is why it is crucial to work fast and not be too precious about the drawings. This merely creates a model of successful motion, however, and does not dramatise the movement through anticipation, characterisation or choreographic effects that would imbue the movement with energy, action, purpose and meaning.

At this point it is important to recognise that a practising animator must both understand the relevance of using life drawing and embrace conventions in animation practice that have essentially become the tricks of the trade. Observation is absolutely crucial even when using the established processes in creating character; beware that some methods produce false energy rather than convincing results.

Animators often first achieve this through their approach to walk cycles, one of the fundamentals of animation practice. Ironically, at one level, a basic walk cycle (see p58–59) is an animation exercise that needs no observation whatsoever and is more of a technical exercise. Crucially, it only becomes observational when we add emotion.

▶

Key poses

artist
Joanna Quinn

A life drawing demonstrating opposite key poses.

Foreshortened image of figure

artist
Joanna Quinn

A figure in a state of repose, but there is still an energy in the posture that suggests the next movement, or a possible reaction to a changing situation. Capturing awareness in drawing is fundamental to successful characterisation.

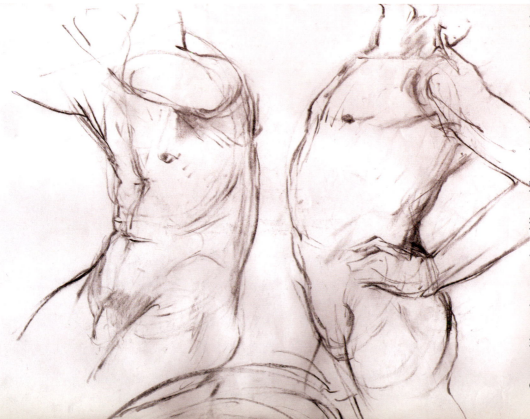

Body parts

The body is a complex and dynamic form and, when illustrated, can be conceived in a variety of ways. Drawing for animation can inevitably be preoccupied with body shape in relation to movement and be less interested in details or, indeed, the variety of postures or positions the physical frame can occupy. These studies by Kimberley Rice reveal how useful it is to cultivate an eye for unusual perspectives, and more detailed sketches of potentially neglected aspects of the bodily form.

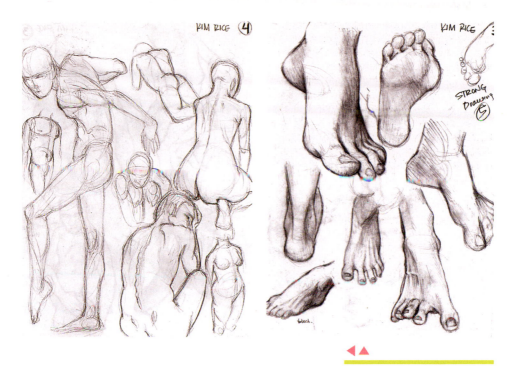

Face studies

artist
Peter Parr

It is important to study and explore facial engagement from a variety of angles as at any one time the human face can express different meanings from different perspectives.

Detailed body part focus

artist
Kimberley Rice

Kimberley Rice captures the sometimes more unusual or less noticed postures and perspectives of the human form. This is crucial to the understanding of the dynamic movement range of the human body, and its ability to configure itself in a variety of complex ways.

As an animator it is necessary to relearn things that are otherwise done instinctively. Each and every apparently simple movement has to be fully analysed for its implicit complexities. How does someone stand up? Walk? Ride a bike? These actions are so simple and so easy that once learned are never thought about again – but it remains important for the animator to consider what these actions are underpinned with, and what was being learned. Essentially, the core aspects to be understood are the principles of gravity and the importance of balance.

Gravity pulls the human form down. Just standing up is a fight against gravity; our natural state would be slumped on the floor. To keep upright humans have to use the appropriate muscles to maintain balance and, for the most part, we do this unconsciously. Babies learn how to stand and walk through trial and error in the same way that we learn to ride a bike intuitively through combining balance, steering and pushing pedals.

▼

Line direction and posture

artist
Joanna Quinn

Quinn points up the postural and emotional imperatives in relation to walking.

Head tilted up above the shoulders

Head tilted down below the shoulders shows real lack of purpose

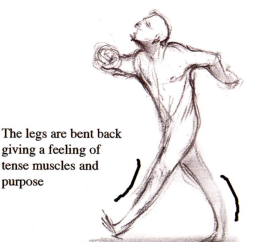

The legs are bent back giving a feeling of tense muscles and purpose

The legs are bent forward giving a feeling of relaxed muscles and floppiness

Body language and walk cycles

Humankind also interprets body language instinctively. By watching the way somebody walks it is possible to know their age, sex, weight, mood and character. Some people are better than others at reading such signs, but an animator must recreate the instinctive nature of body language because an audience will immediately spot if the animation does not ring true and characters seem unpersuasive and two dimensional.

Body language signals effectively govern the way that humans present themselves to other people and animals, eg the way people hold their hands in front of them can sometimes seem self-protective or defensive; the way a person might tap a foot or jiggle a leg might be viewed as a sign of nervousness; blinking too much could be a sign of lying – people interpret such signs without even thinking. It is crucial to embed this within the animation.

Basic walk cycle rules

No straight lines – choose a direction for each line. Each line needs to be complementary and bend in the pertinent direction.

Don't draw the joints or construct the body out of balls. Feel the whole body as a bean shape and draw the legs and arms as continuous forms like spaghetti. This eliminates straight lines and helps the animator to think more loosely and about the movement, rather than the anatomical make-up.

No clothes and no cartoon conventions – make the drawing as free a representation as possible in the first instance. Any attempt to draw a realistic body conjures up the image of an anatomically correct figure. Such conventions detract from the clarity of the direction of the line in describing parts of the body.

Head and neck straight and above the shoulders looks wooden

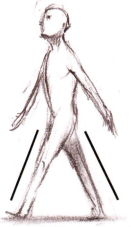

The legs are straight giving a feeling of being rigid and unnatural

Basic walk cycle

The basic walk cycle is in many senses the touchstone in developing expression of motion, and operates as proof of a mastery of essential movement structures before attempting more complex choreography in the drawn form.

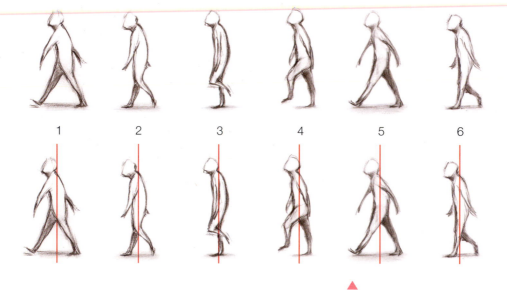

▲

Basic walk cycle

animator
Joanna Quinn

with the centre line inserted – the centre line being an imagined line through the body to help define its potential symmetries and shifts from a pivotal balancing place.

Joanna Quinn's basic walk cycle

'This is a basic walk cycle that I do. It could do with one extra drawing between each key to make it slower and more natural, but it works fine as it stands.'

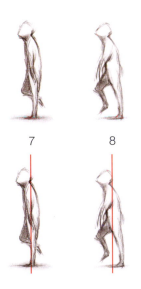

7   8

Order of the drawings

There are eight drawings in a cycle, completed in the following order.

▶ I start with number 1.

▶ Then I do number 5 by tracing over 1, but swapping the legs and arms round so the left leg and right arm lead the way.

▶ Then I do number 3, which is an in-between of 1 and 5. I always put the first drawings in the sequence underneath, so number 5 is over number 1. Although this drawing is an in-between, the leg that is in contact with the ground is straight so the body needs to lift higher up.

▶ Next I do number 7, which is just a tracing of number 3 but with the legs and arms swapped around.

▶ Then I put the drawings in order and put 1 and 3 on the light box and draw the in-between, which will be number 2. 1 and 2 get put on the 'finished' pile.

▶ Then number 3 and number 5 are put on the light box and I draw the in-between number 4. 3 and 4 get put on the 'finished' pile.

▶ Then I do an in-between of 5 and 7. This will be number 6. 5 and 6 go to the 'finished' pile.

▶ Then I do an in-between of 7 and 1. This will be number 8 and the cycle is complete.

The cycle can be made more natural and fluid by making the head bob slightly. If you act out an over-exaggerated walk and make your head quite floppy you notice that it mirrors the up-and-down rhythm of the body, but with a slight delay. For instance, drawing number 3 actually has drawing number 2's head.

The language of full animation – the process of capturing the seemingly natural but invisible complexity of physical expression – was constructed during the 'golden era' of Disney, and has been passed on to, and modified by, contemporary master animators such as Glen Keane. In thinking animation, the animator is concerned with matching carefully observed physical movement with its apparent motivation and purpose.

Peter Parr outlines ten core principles for thinking about animating through drawing.

All artwork in this section is by Peter Parr.

> Movement is not simply watching a subject in motion; the structure of a drawing can convey movement by navigating the viewer's eye across its surface in two or three dimensions.
>
> Peter Parr

1   Reference

Research your subject matter thoroughly before choosing an appropriate style for your animation.

▲ ◀

Two key areas for exploration and record are depictions of animals and distinctive places. To be able to draw animals is to exhibit a strong sense of anatomical knowledge and gestural understanding. Capturing the specificity of places, too, can be useful in creating distinctive and attractive layouts.

Practice

2   Line and volume
Develop a rapid and fluid line technique to express volume.

▼

Parr presents volume through the intensity or lightness of his line forms. These animals take on weight and spatial effect through the choices in line idioms and applications.

3   Tone and texture
When you apply tone and texture, force your eye and hand to imitate the surface of your subject.

▲▼

Parr expresses texture through tonal variations in light and colour, suggesting, in these images, the silkiness in the period costume and the roughness of the bark of an old oak tree.

Movement and dynamics > **Thinking animation** > Drawing characters

4 Structure and weight
Look for pressure points and angles in the subject (contrapositions) before adding detail.

5 Movement and rhythm
Keep your eye alert and darting to every part of your drawing, including the parts unseen.

▲▼

It is important to consider the structure and weight not only of the human body, but also of elemental and organic forms like the sea, and the particular conditions of buildings and environments; doing so authenticates the illusionism available through drawing.

▲

Movement and rhythm are fundamental to successful animation and are endemic in the performances of dancers (see the work of Erica Russell later in this book) and the natural motion of animals.

Practice

6 Gesture

One single line should define the characteristic of your subject – optimistic, pessimistic, or resolute.

7 Energy (angry or passive)

Look closely at your subject and for the energy it conveys, and draw that before any detail.

▲▼

Parr's images demonstrate that gesture is not merely a physically intended act, but a signature part of particular movements and postures. Gesture is in effect the best expression of attitude and feeling and an extremely important tool in the animator's armoury as an actor and performer.

▲▼

Parr depicts the aggression and passion in a rugby match, and the sense of patience and preoccupation in a passenger waiting for a flight. Crucially, although one scenario has more self-evident action, energy is still reflected in the attitude and posture of the less active figure.

Movement and dynamics > **Thinking animation** > Drawing characters

8   Balance and composition
Respect the whole page before balancing your drawing on its surface.

▲▼

Everyday scenes take on aesthetic and narrative purpose when the mise-en-scène is composed to suggest context or imminent action. Engaging environments can be particularly important as extra 'characters' – an issue explored later in the book.

9   Narrative and sequence
To create a prehistory and a future for your drawing, try to capture a single moment in time.

▲

Parr suggests narrative possibility through the actions of his characters – essentially 'the text' – and uses comic-book conventions in the form of think bubbles to communicate the subtext of the scene. He captures narrative and possible sequential action in Portland Fair, which is further dramatised through his use of dynamic colour. Action and attitude are implicit in each scene, providing possible stimuli for narrative development.

10 Perspective

Put simply – foreground large, distance small – perspective allows you to reach into the page.

▲ ▼

Parr's sketch of the Great Wall of China shows an incline that is actually going into the distance: this is a reversal of the convention in many cartoons where roads veer away downhill and into the distance. The Viborg street depicted below does this but, like the Wall, still suggests the possibility of action to follow.

Glen Keane's selected 'animation notes' are as follows:

Don't illustrate words or mechanical movements. Illustrate ideas or thoughts, with attitudes and actions.

Squash and stretch the entire body for attitudes.

If possible, make definite changes from one attitude to another in timing and expression.

Always ask: 'What is the character thinking?'

It is the thought and circumstances behind an action that will make the action interesting.

Don't move anything unless it is for a purpose.

Concentrate on drawing clear, not clean.

Everything has a function. Don't draw without knowing why.

Think in terms of drawing the whole character, not just the head or eyes, etc. Keep a balanced relationship between one part of the drawing and another.

Stage for the most effective drawing.

Movement and dynamics > **Thinking animation** > Drawing characters

The ground rules and conceptual guidelines discussed previously may be tested further by changing the nature, dynamic and purpose of an action sequence. One method is to use the initial basic walk cycle as a guide underneath new walk cycles; however, the new walk requires planning, as it is in effect the first attempt to characterise or dramatise the walk. Acting through the drawn form is paramount in this as the character must emerge from within the motion, his emotion described through his energy, poise and speed and how he carries his weight. This, in turn, requires a further exploration of three-dimensional space and the movement and possible rotation of the figure through an implied environment.

Inevitably, different parts of the body will move with different timing, and this can help define the character – an aspect that can be further enhanced through exaggeration of the motion itself – and the perspective from which the figure is observed. This is invariably related to the emotional state underpinning the walk – joyful, optimistic strides will differ from a depressed lope; a tired body will perform more slowly than the agitated, possibly staccato expression of an angry figure; a drunk, unable to control his movement, will differ from the precision and focus of someone deliberately managing the movement in a broken or wounded leg.

▲

Character sketch – Bev from Body Beautiful

artist
Joanna Quinn

Quinn's character studies give a ready indication of the ways in which characters may move, and how, in essence, they dramatise their emotions and outlooks.

Practice

Creating a simple walk cycle and engaging in preliminary controlled acting serves as the basis for a more complicated sequence that includes a series of actions that will bring a character alive. Crucial in this is the timing of the separate actions working together for best effect; if the timing is wrong all the hard work that has been put into the animation goes unnoticed. The gaps between the actions are as important as the actions themselves. Fundamental to successful timing is making sure the key poses are strong and clear opposites; this makes the animation so much more interesting and the acting specific and punctuated.

The key action for each movement needs to be identified and its timing initially worked out: for a walk cycle this concerns the timing of the primary stride then the secondary actions that subsequently follow it; for example, the swing of the arms, the slightly delayed bob of the head, the hair shift, etc. For more complex actions, these movements might be primary actions in themselves, and not merely the consequence of a primary action.

It is important to check the arc of a movement at all points from its inception through to its conclusion. This enables the proper identification of where the centre of balance is in the drawing of a figure: when somebody is falling forward or back they need to be well beyond the centre of gravity. An important point to note is that less attention should be paid to facial expression here as it can become a short cut that undermines the expression of emotion made fully through the body.

Drawings inevitably have to be reworked to properly execute these principles, so all drawings should be seen as part of a process and none held as singularly important or definitive.

Dog walk cycle

artist
Animation Workshop

In this comic walk cycle the core actions of the dog's torso moving up and down and the forward leg cycle are easily observed, but crucial to the comic aspect of the sequence are the secondary actions of the ears, tongue, eyes and tail, which also move back and forth but in opposing or arbitrary directions.

Miming techniques

Mime is an extremely useful tool in helping to identify movement arcs and in providing definition. The use of mime technique demands that the actor's bodily movements describe the object. For example, in the case of throwing a ball, the mime of the action must demonstrate the pathway of the ball not only through the projection of the ball with the hands and arms, and the follow-through of the limbs, but how the eyes and head follow the action. In another example – tripping over an object – the body is thrown off-balance; in falling or attempting to save the body from a fall, the physical actions radically change, and in the recovery the body can be seen to come back to its former state of equilibrium. This action has become a moment of dramatisation and a complex expression of emotion and physical control/lack of control. Vitally, the animator must remember that no matter how out of control the action depicted is, its expression must always be controlled.

In the animated form, it is important to secure the action and its extremes before thinking about the lip-sync. Lip-sync, though thought of as merely the synchronisation of mouth movement with the intended dialogue, is actually about acting with the body and the face; the lips, ironically, are the least important element. The primary action is the bodily expression, then facial expression and the work of the eyes. Secondary animation – the work of the mouth – should be added last. In this respect, work should start with broad strokes perfecting the overall timing and body gestures in relation to the significant points in a sound; only then should the focus move to the gestural detail. The emphasis in the soundtrack will determine where the primary key drawings go.

Digger

artist
Joanna Quinn

Quinn's depiction of Digger in *Dreams and Desires: Family Ties* (2006) not merely captures the dynamic animal but a character who contributes to the narrative through his own actions and the ways he is acted upon.

Inevitably, capturing the work of facial expressions requires practice, and extensive observation of models and people in everyday life. Depicting emotion or physical states – surprise, fear, drunkenness, anger, concern, etc – requires paying special attention to the body, eyebrows, eyes, mouth and forehead. The expressions of different emotions are sometimes quite similar (for example, anger and confusion), so it is necessary to pinpoint what the difference is and to give it particular emphasis in the drawing. Once this emotional range has been addressed, then the technical aspects of executing mouth shapes should be looked at. Watching a model deliver vowels and consonants is very helpful in this regard.

For the character animator, the capture of facial expression and physical movement is completely instrumental in the construction of character. Many animators hone their skills in this area first by observing animals. Because so many animals feature in films from the United States, it is important to truly observe the animal in order to avoid slipping into the clichés of animal representation already established by countless cartoons. Animal observation remains pertinent for drawing, however, because animals express themselves almost purely through their physical presence and actions.

In traditional scripts, the human character often has a profile, and may be understood through his actions and his dialogue throughout the story, ie his character is deduced from text and interpreted accordingly. In animation, characters are often defined first through their design – in model sheets, action sketches, etc – and are therefore informed by their physical demeanour and actions first. Characterisation is first and foremost, though, not who a character is, but what a character does. It is crucial, therefore, to identify the traits within a personality that makes a character recognisable and readily visualised. By looking at animals, prospective animators need to identify what it is that makes that animal so recognisably true in and of itself.

Once the soundtrack has been heard over and over again, the animator should identify the key expressive words, and begin to use a **dope sheet** to notate the planning of the vocal expression in relation to its animation. Wherever the animator thinks the delivery is at its most exaggerated or extreme, this will be where the corresponding key frames should go. Again, such a sequence should be executed first as a thumbnail storyboard, and the sound matched to it as quickly as possible, however inexact and unspecific. The proper timing of the action is crucial in that it must ultimately match the timing of the vocal delivery. A line-tester should be used to carefully match the timings of the key drawings against the sound; the drawings can then be numbered and entered on the dope sheet. It will then become clear how many in-betweens are necessary. This normally leads to the identification of key sub-poses/vocal actions that define the complete movement. Once all the main drawings are in place and timed out, the mouth movement and the last in-betweens can be executed, and follow-on animation, eg hair and floppy elements, can be completed. At all points, reference should be made to the developmental drawings of the animals/characters.

Practice

Dope sheet a planning tool for animators that allows all intended visualised action and sound to be broken down by frame, scene and sequence to provide instructions to the rest of the team. Also known as an exposure sheet or a camera-instruction sheet.

▶ ▼

Mouth studies

artist
Kimberley Rice

Kimberley Rice here gives consideration to when the cat opens its mouth, recognising that lip-syncing is pertinent to the movement of the animal overall. In her sketches of some of the characters from Disney's *Sword in the Stone* (1963), she considers mouth positions as expressive indicators in advance of lip-sync.

The production processes under consideration in this chapter promote drawing as a facilitator as well as a mediator of ideas. If the Disney classical style prioritised the presentation of personality and conviction through drawing, many of the procedural models that follow use drawing as a tool towards manifesting an idea through an expressive, graphic or illustrative strategy. Despite the common assumption that the computer has taken over the roles that once informed animation, it is clear that drawing still provides the platform for much of the work, and readily underpins all aspects of choreographing and sustaining animation itself in any technique or style.

Drawing can both simplify and complicate, reduce and amplify an idea, and, in whatever context, can be applied in a way that defines what might be understood as the architecture of a narrative; a visual premise; a character or environment; a point of view or perspective (material or metaphorical); and, most significantly, the form of expression. When drawing provides the infrastructure of an approach there is always a relationship between the psychology of creative practice and its technical applications.

title
Azur and Asmar

animator
Michel Ocelot

Every project requires an 'inciting idea' – the core idea that prompts a creative process. This first major idea needs to be developed through research and testing, but eventually finds a creative context after it has been modified and fully explored. In animation this is intrinsically related to the way the idea can be visualised and in what technique, and through what process, it will be developed. Interestingly, no matter what technique or approach is actually chosen, it is usually the case, whether the piece is being created through a formal script or evolving through a more improvised or fluid process, that drawing is in some way involved.

Les Mills notes: 'My big thing about animation was the concept, the ideas, and the lack of fear – trying to get students not to be afraid of exploring their ideas, and the graphic qualities that they all had. That was the thing I brought to the teaching of animation.' Throughout his working career with Joanna Quinn, he has constantly stressed that films should be clearly 'about' something, noting for example: 'Britannia is pretty obviously about anti-colonialism, anti-imperialism by anybody, but particularly focused on Britain. But it could apply to Spain, Portugal, France – America now, I guess. The main line of it is exploitation by large nations of small nations, and colonisation. And Elles is really about painting.' As part of the development of Body Beautiful, Mills enhanced the notion of the 'inciting idea' with further objectives:

▶ To give a more defined and enduring identity to the character of Beryl and others in the film, but in particular to establish Beryl as a genuine anti-heroine.

▶ To construct a narrative that reflected the changing role of women at work and the decline of heavy local industry generally.

▶ To use the whole structure of the film as a metaphor for political and military struggles between small underprivileged nations and oppressive powerful ones.

▶ To use dialogue improvisation by key actors as a tool for script development and refinement.

▶ To use research as a major background informing ingredient in mise-en-scène.

▶ To exploit Joanna's ability to create enduring and distinctive characters and to fully exploit her immense natural drawing and brilliant animating capabilities.

Mills explores the 'inciting idea' of *Dreams and Desires: Family Ties* later, as part of a range of examples here that show aspects of the animation production process that are specifically related to the role and function of drawing, even as they inform different styles. When the 'inciting idea' comes, it is normally through drawing that it is formulated and advanced, and this can occur only at the outset of a project, or throughout its whole duration. Each project discussed here stresses how drawing helps formulate ideas, and uses particular applications of drawing to enable the work to come to full fruition.

◀

title
Whiskas advertisement

artist
Joanna Quinn

Some creatures plot, while others dream. Plotting and dreaming are fundamental to creative work!

The inciting idea > Script

The linear journey to digital drawing

All projects begin with a particular idea or point of stimulus, but in this context it is important to explore how drawing might work. Michael Shaw, for example, uses drawing as a tool in relation to digital screen practice. Here he addresses his work:

'For over a decade drawing has complemented my practice as a sculptor, primarily through form generation, occasionally to problem-solve and more often than not as an activity in its own right. Since 2006 much sculpture has been manifested through computer-aided design and manufacture, in turn prompting a series of animated drawings that attempt to bridge the divide between two and three dimensions.

'In a traditional drawing the viewer usually only sees the final outcome and is excluded from the **process** of its making unless some faintly rubbed-out or smudged traces of its history remain visible. Alternatively, through animation, the process of laying down a drawn image can be revealed so that form slowly comes to fruition. My process of creating the animated drawings subverts the usual progression towards refined form in drawn media on paper; instead, virtual forms are modelled and then lines of motion are bound to their surfaces to determine the flow of brushstrokes that then draw each form progressively. These constructions are therefore sculpted drawings.

'*What Might Be* (2006) explores one of the fundamental aims of drawing, if not art in general: how to project the illusion of three-dimensional space into the planar. The latter is especially relevant to the sculptor and, intriguingly, animation appears well placed to recreate the perambulatory and kinetic nature of experiencing sculpture by manipulating the observer's viewpoint by proxy. It therefore unites the second and fourth dimensions to imply the third.

'*What Might Be* shares much in common with traditional drawing materials and seeks life-like depictions of media including pencil, rubber, charcoal, wax resist, pen and ink and the potential subtlety of marks such as smudges, overdrawing, traces, and bleeds. Layer upon layer of virtual material is overlaid until the stained history of its making emerges.

'Whilst the translation from paper to screen provides no answers, it does create opportunities for the act of drawing to become visible over time, kinetic, complex and sustained through the light of projection or back-lit screening.'

Process drawing can reveal the thought processes behind the act of creativity, as well as the experience of the artist as the drawing unfolds, as seen in the work of Michael Shaw and William Kentridge.

My process of creating the animated drawings subverts the usual progression towards refined form in drawn media on paper; instead, virtual forms are modelled and then lines of motion are bound to their surfaces to determine the flow of brushstrokes that then draw each form progressively. These constructions are therefore sculpted drawings.

Michael Shaw

title
What Might Be

artist
Michael Shaw

Michael Shaw successfully transcends the 2D/3D divide by privileging the techniques of drawing as aesthetic principles in themselves, foregrounding them within an emergent, animated environment.

The inciting idea > Script

Drawing and film language

Les Mills, Joanna Quinn's long-time scriptwriter and collaborator, has remained consistently preoccupied with his own engagement with film and film language, and Quinn's highly developed skills in drawing. Les says:

'Part of the structural concept of *Dreams and Desires: Family Ties* was that the central character, Beryl, would become a mature film student, engaging in the process of understanding film language, theory, and cinema generally, through a practical process of discovery, ie learning from books, watching classic DVDs and finally using her digicam to explore herself, her ideas and the medium itself. This would be the birth of Beryl as Renaissance woman and would additionally engage other cultural forms, in particular the visual arts and, to some extent, literature.'

title
**Dreams and Desires:
Family Ties**

artist
Joanna Quinn

Quinn uses images to sustain a narrative and to call attention to the ways in which drawing has been used in fine art compositionally, aesthetically and metaphorically. The cherubs that feature in Beryl's fantasies recall Rubenesque caricatures and some of the symbolic dynamics of Renaissance art forms. Other examples here show the vitality and mobility within the mise-en-scène of the image, and draw attention to animation's particular quality in specifically creating imagery unattainable in other approaches.

'Other viewpoints were adopted when Beryl was deliberately trying out shots in homage to seminal film-makers, eg the tracking shot in the church that imitated Leni Riefenstahl's direction in such films as *Triumph of the Will* (1935) and *Olympia* (1938), and mounting the camera on Digger the dog's back to make direct reference to Dziga Vertov's dynamic use of camera viewpoint and position in his *Kino-pravda* series.'

'The other major structural basis for *Dreams and Desires* is Beryl's conversion into a diarist, someone who continuously engages herself and her audience in a continuing examination of her personal philosophies, relationships, universal themes and, of course, the film-making process itself. We deliberately limited aspects of the **mise-en-scène** to make Beryl a prisoner of the camera in as much as she could only operate within the range of subjective camera shots, ie from her own point of view or directly engaging herself in front of the camera.'

Mise-en-scène the nature and construction of the material content of the image. In animation, the normal conventions of the physical and performance space are in flux so that animated events – a gag, a specific image, an abstract form, etc – stand out.

Les Mills continues:

'Digger the dog's name is a somewhat oblique homage to Dziga Vertov, and his canine meanderings at the wedding reception are an overt reference to his *Man with a Movie Camera* (1929) transposed into *Dog with a Movie Camera*. Joanna slipped in a playful and whimsical scene outside the church where the bride throws her bouquet and Digger leaps in and steals it, then destroys it. Because this scene was improvised and not scripted I chose to reference Cecil Hepworth's *Rescued by Rover* (1905), one of the first films which played with broken or simultaneous film narrative and which sowed the seeds of narrative language in cinema so brilliantly exploited by DW Griffith. To make the reference slightly more obvious I had to write some lines for Beryl reminding Digger that he hadn't seen that film.'

Mills's engagement with film language reveals the limits of traditional live-action 'recording' of actuality, and the freer, more open mise-en-scène of animated forms. With each use of animation there demonstrates the particular qualities of the drawn form in exhibiting the distinctive aspects of animation as a language, cited in the box below.

title
**Dreams and Desires:
Family Ties**

artist
Joanna Quinn

The scene outside the church in which Digger catches a bouquet and tears it apart takes on further resonance when grounded in ironic references to other image systems. The film uses animation generally to imitate yet refresh numerous taken-for-granted professional and amateur approaches to composition and literal record.

The language of animation

Remember, animation has a specific and particular language of expression that is at the heart of some of its distinctive approaches. Here are its core characteristics:

Metamorphosis
The ability to facilitate the change from one form into another without edit.

Condensation
The maximum degree of suggestion in the minimum of imagery.

Anthropomorphism
The imposition of human traits on animals, objects and environments.

Fabrication
The physical and material creation of imaginary figures and spaces.

Penetration
The visualisation of unimaginable psychological/physical/technical interiors.

Symbolic association
The use of abstract visual signs and their related meanings.

Sound illusion
The completely artificial construction of a soundtrack to support the intrinsic silence of animated forms.

Drawing and abstraction

Experimental film-maker Clive Walley uses drawing as a way of conceptualising his ideas but, unusually, develops them within prose pieces, exploring and describing his creative thoughts and possible applications. His film *Light of Uncertainty* (1998) is a reflection upon the art and science of expressing abstract formulation, and both his preparatory work and the animation itself are an interpretation and illustration of theoretical principles.

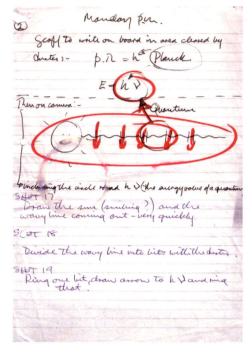

title
Light of Uncertainty

artist
Clive Walley

Walley considers the way in which an equation can be introduced and shown visually, using the terms and conditions of scientific expression as a means to aesthetic extrapolation. His address of quantum physics, and the nature and frequency of light forms, is both the subject and object of the animation. The calculation and expression of this theory generates his visual ideas.

to draw around where the leg should be. Then I cut them out. Problem is that when a leg disappears for a long while it has to be in the right place when it reappears or there will be a jump to the proper place when the leg becomes visible again.

I used an overlay and a soluble marker to draw positions at beginning and end – just before leg disappears and just after it reappears, – and in betweened from that. Very fiddly. All one day mounting the copies on cell and drawing in where legs ought to be. Another day cutting out and testing. 109 drawings altogether.

BUT THEY LOOK GREAT.

They are on the tape where they would go to make steps 13 + 14 + 15. The gap between the steps seen in back proj + the appearance of the photocopied legs under water might now be covered thus :–

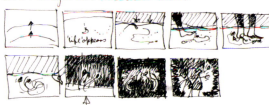

Here the visible blobs fly up into the dark which has to convincingly become the light very quickly as the back proj comes in.

There are a variety of methods for generating a script for an animated film. The animator could work with a traditional script, predicated on written descriptors and dialogue or, equally, might work purely through visualisation processes, such as sketching and storyboarding, or even through pure improvisation with particular materials and techniques. Each approach is informed by different intentions and, inevitably, will have different outcomes. What remains significant, however, is the place that drawing has in these scriptwriting approaches, and its common presence as part of virtually every project, whatever the style or approach.

In many ways it was drawing in the first instance that suggested the distinctive ways in which animation could work with symbols and signs as visual short cuts in the representation of human beings, animals, objects and, crucially, ideas and concepts. This offered up the possibility of picturing invisible or seemingly unimaginable things, whether they be complicated theorems or interior psychological, organic, material or mechanical states. Drawing enabled the specific selection of an idea or form to be expressed, and in that allowed for it to be exaggerated, minimalised or transformed altogether.

Once drawings began to move in animation, the additional dimension of time enabled drawing to reveal the past or project towards a future, and to be part of the ways in which animation could seemingly control all aspects of the temporal order or spatial configuration. Drawing – like other materials used in animation – could enable metamorphosis (the seemingly seamless transition from one state or form to another); condensation (the maximum of suggestion in the minimum of imagery); fabrication (the creation of imaginary orders, environments and worlds); and, importantly, offered a vehicle for visualisation that was inherently metaphorical and metaphysical. Another title in this series, *Basics Animation: Scriptwriting*, provides a fuller discussion of this topic.

title
John and Michael

animator
Shira Avni

National Film Board of Canada artist Shira Avni suggests compositional and motion aspects within the frame to instigate a sense of how the animation itself will eventually work. The looseness and suggestiveness of the line itself is highly pertinent in showing aspects of both the physical and spiritual flight in the characters.

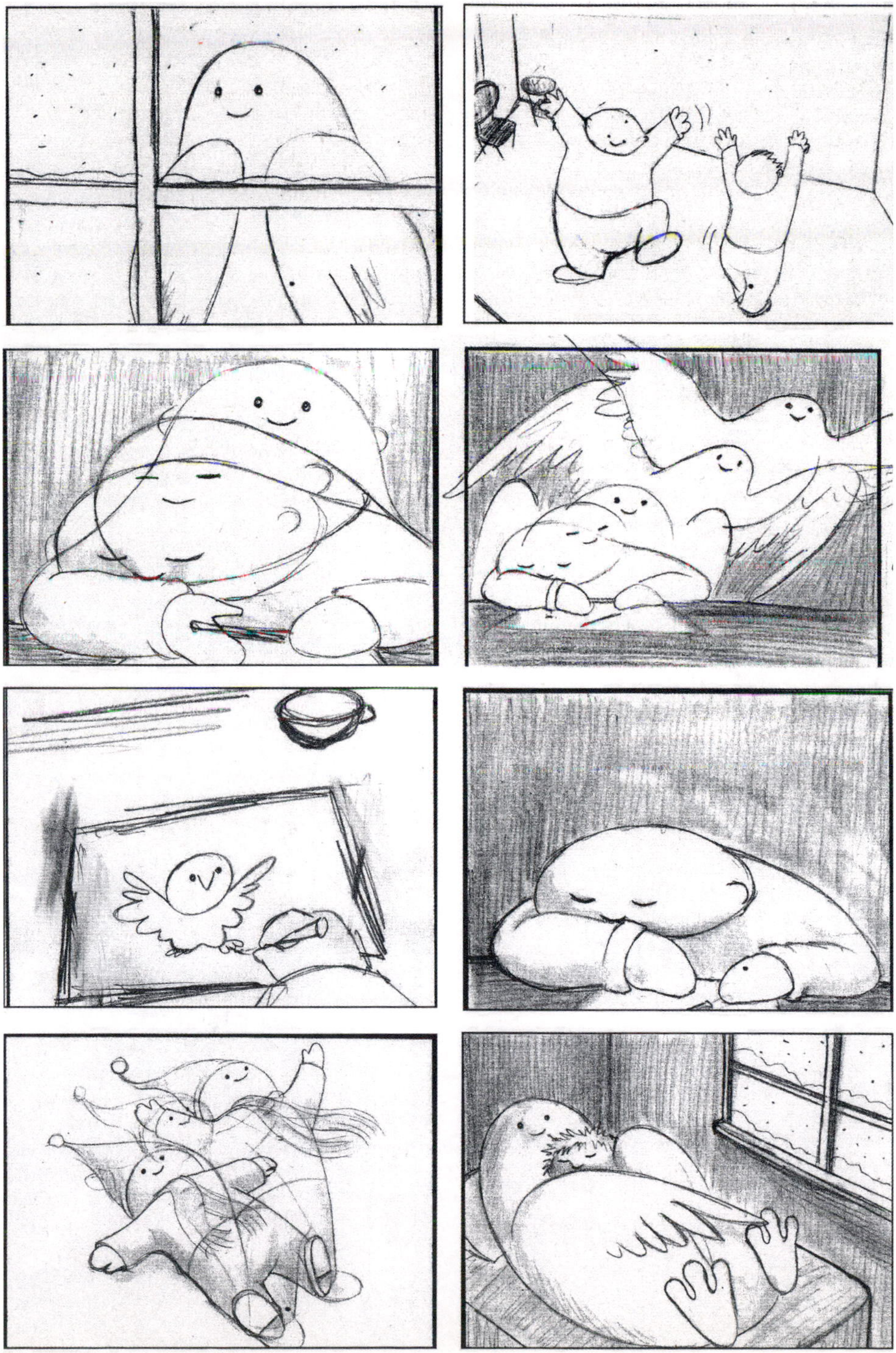

Former animator and visual developer at Amblimation and Warner Bros. Feature Animation, Julia Bracegirdle, is particularly interested in storyboarding and in teaching **visualisation** through this approach. She believes that the storyboard should be understood and defined in the following way:

'A storyboard is the sequential ordering of panels (or individual pictures) that illustrate and sustain narrative momentum; in a sense it is a visual script and, much like a script, it goes through many drafts. Storyboarding is also a pre-production visualising tool that helps to define the look of a film. And it is a way of coming up with new visual and narrative ideas before production or shooting begins. As a production planning tool, the storyboard enables the organisation of the content of shots and what work needs to be done; and together with the animatic (a filmed and timed version of the storyboard), it is a blueprint for the film that will be referred to by all throughout production.'

These are storyboards produced for Right Angle Productions' collaborative project, *Animated World Faiths* (1998) for SC4. Work was produced both in Wales and across various European studios, and the storyboards reflect the ways in which the collaboration took place, first as a response to the provisional script, second, in relation to the most persuasive visualisation of the material in relation to the narrative, and third, as a proposal of how the material should be shot.

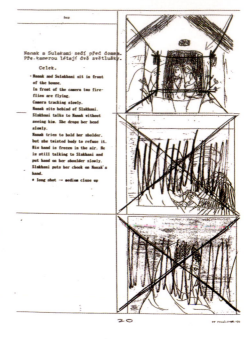

title
**Animated World Faiths
(The Story of Guru Nanak)**

animator
Right Angle Productions

Different kinds of drawing represent different stages of thought and points of representation. Sometimes, there is a sense of the portrait, which privileges the close-up (top); sometimes graphic forms such as a map are used (middle); on other occasions there are different models of staging and shooting for the same scene, with varying levels of emphasis (bottom).

Visualisation stresses only the pictorial and works differently to, or complementarily with, dialogue and written descriptors. Visualisation processes are determined by the technique chosen, the concept engaged with and the intention of the narrative.

hra

· Nanak opens his eyes.
  * medium close up
  [dissolve]
Nanak otvírá oči.
Polodetail.
Prolínačka.

· A map appears. It shows Nanak's
  journey.
Objeví se mapa. Ukazuje Nanakovy
cesty.
Detail staršího Nanaka. Káže lidem.
Kamera transfok. a pan. doprava.
Na tesařovu dílnu. Tesař dělá
truhlu. Přestane a dívá se na Nanaka.
    69
· Long shot. Nanak preaches to the
  people. Camera zoom in slowly.
    69 a
· Lalo makes plain wooden box. We
  see Nanak over him. They look at
  each other. Malik Bhago and his
  servent close to Nanak.

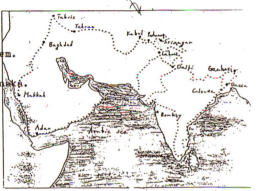

Malik Bhago

29

Bracegirdle's storyboard essentials

A storyboard is :

About removing and replacing panels in order to improve the visual script.

About drawing, redrawing and redrawing and redrawing.

About improvisation and experimentation when it is cheap and fast to do so.

Avoiding good paper or sketchbooks; both promote the precious attitude it is crucial not to have.

Breaking down the narrative into all the necessary shots or scenes that tell the story.

Creating a first thumbnail run-through about character and plot, not composition and camera moves, in the first instance.

Recognising how every panel affects what may or may not happen next in the narrative.

Reflection, which allows better illustration of the narrative by shaping and rearranging the running order of storyboard panels.

An image sequence that can be used to construct 'animatics'.

title
**Animated World Faiths
(The Story of Guru Nanak)**

animator
Right Angle Productions

The storyboard can be used as a significant problem-solving tool; drawing represents the thinking process as it addresses the issues that arise – correcting, editing, redrawing, making compositional selection, etc.

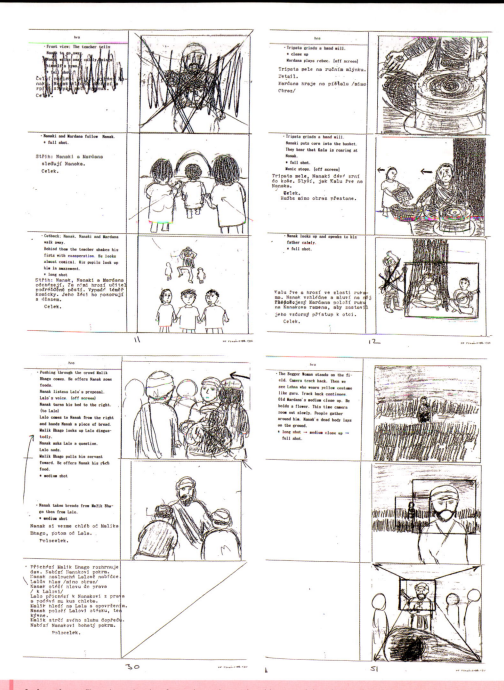

Animatics a filmed synthesis of storyboard panels with a provisional soundtrack to create a mock version of the animation. This is used to gauge if the narrative works, what might need to be added or removed, and how the dialogue, music, etc might potentially work in relation to the suggested images.

Scenes

In relation to drawing, scenes are less about the nature of dramatisation and performance and more concerned with background, **layout** and choreography: the context in which narrative, characters and action develop. Though it is easy to become preoccupied by performance and dialogue in dramatic scenes, contextualisation within animation is important in creating meaning and effect.

Two examples follow: A. Film's *Terkel in Trouble* (2004) and Quentin Marmier's *Oktapodi* (2007).

Terkel in Trouble

With director Kresten Andersen's *Terkel in Trouble*, A. Film wished to make an edgy, economically viable feature film that would appeal directly to a teenage audience. A. Film wanted to innovate in computer-generated work through its design strategy, using the limitations of its means as a prompt to be more inventive. A scaled-down team forced an optimised workflow and all the characters were based on the same core design, with greater focus on the story, voice-acting, and humour of the piece. This directly echoes Hanna-Barbera's strategy in the mid-1950s when developing television cartoons such as *Ruff 'n' Reddy* and *The Huckleberry Hound Show*, when it was no longer cost-effective to produce shorts for theatrical distribution.

Drawing in a less elaborate way liberates the animator to take short cuts, reuse cycles and generally create a rougher, less developed aesthetic. In *Terkel in Trouble*, this enabled key framing to be combined with simple motion capture and automated compositing set-ups.

Andersen was influenced by *The Muppet Show*, *The Simpsons* and, most particularly, *South Park*, and sought to create a radical version of the children's story that would abandon Disney-style sentimentality and moral trauma and reflect some of the indifference, cruelty and abandon of children's relationships to each other.

Layout provides a background to the action, and may also offer a mapping or performative element if shot in a specific way. Layout is a pertinent aspect of visualisation when allied to choreographed moves.

title
Terkel in Trouble

animator
A. Film

The initial character sketches demonstrate the core shape of the characters. Like the Ub Iwerks designs for the early *Silly Symphonies* in the 1920s, the approach is based on 'rope' limbs and primary circle or oblong shapes for faces and bodies, with differentiation achieved through slight reconfigurations in hair, eye, nose and mouth styling.

Terkel's town and its geographic perspective are delineated to convey a sense of the small world of the characters, where Terkel's home, the school and the village hall, and even the woodlands are all close together.

CHARACTER SKETCHES 2

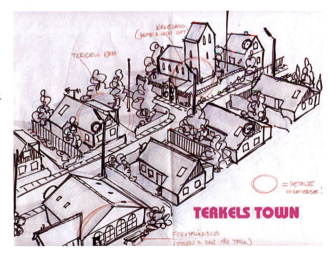

TERKELS TOWN

PLAN VIEW

Terkel in Trouble also uses a limited number of environments – mainly domestic interiors, small-scale venues and suggestions of exterior sites such as the woodland camp. The preparatory drawings for these environments work not merely as designs for the spaces but as a map of the Terkel world, communicating a full understanding of the limited choreographies required, and the concentration upon character action and dialogue within spaces, rather than a particular need for the environment to contribute in a highly significant way.

A. Film's intention to limit the drawn aesthetic of the piece directly eased the translation of the design into digital form. Whereas in computer-generated animation the drawings that inform the creation of characters are of an 'inspirational' nature, or are part of a particular portfolio by any one animator or designer, in this instance the drawing almost works as a direct template for the computer-generated characters.

title
Terkel in Trouble

animator
A. Film

Various characters from *Terkel in Trouble* in their drawn and computer-generated forms. Only minor modifications in the design occur, largely related to configurations of the mouth and play with hairstyles.

Oktapodi

Oktapodi, created by Quentin Marmier and his colleagues, Julien Bocabeille, François-Xavier Chanioux, Olivier Delabarre, Thierry Marchand and Emud Mokhberi, is an engaging cartoon that features a fishmonger chasing two escaped octopi. This brief description in no way reflects the dynamism and invention of the piece, which benefits greatly from the ways in which the backstreet intricacies of the small seaside town and the construction of the buildings operate effectively as characters in the chase.

Marmier explains: 'The development process was the same as a CG feature animation in a bigger studio with the difference that we were seven people (including the composer) doing everything. We started with the writing of the scenario using some technical and artistic aspects we wanted to see in the film. Then we began pre-production (concepts, colours, design style) and drawing the storyboard in parallel with this.

title
Oktapodi

animator
Marmier et al.

Like the designers on Pixar's *Finding Nemo* (2003), the *Oktapodi* team had limited means to create personality in the sea creatures. Thoughts and feelings are communicated through the eyes and the gestural specificity of the tentacles.

Oktapodi was the group's first experience of producing computer-generated animation and was informed by viewing the previous year's graduation films and the influence of current features by Pixar, DreamWorks and Blue Sky Film. Crucially, though, Marmier and his colleagues engaged in detailed research, not merely by embracing the design of Chris Wedge's *Ice Age* (2002), but by tracing the work of character designer Peter de Sève and examining his portfolio across a number of projects. This proved invaluable when thinking about drawing styles and translating them into computer-generated imagery.

Marmier points out: 'I think that drawing is still the basis of everything…. People who have drawing skills are the best to address limitations and respond to constraints. Whatever you touch as a creative practice, drawing underpins it in some way, and using drawing as an approach is something you just can't get rid of. It is the same for animation. People used to think that new computer technology would make drawing obsolete, but we just have to look at the different major 3D animation studios like Pixar or DreamWorks to see that drawing is still present at each step of the production: concept, storyboard, lighting, etc.'

title
Oktapodi

animator
Marmier et al.

The fishmonger/sailor's van tumbles into the sea following its chase through the descending townscape.

title
Oktapodi

animator
Marmier et al.

The rendered images for *Oktapodi* illustrate the clear influence of classical animation styling in the colour palette and choreography, but also show great command of the techniques required to translate classic styling into computer-generated form.

The Disney style is just one kind of drawing that appears in the final image. CG features are using the same production pipeline as Disney, but they are just adding a different process to build the final images; a technological process. It is important to view the current computer-generated aesthetic as intrinsically related to Disney's classical form, even though the sophistication of visual effects can distract from the formative function of drawing in the development of the work.

Recent animation production has been characterised by the use of 3D computer animation, and even artists who have worked in more traditional forms now seek to embrace its possibilities, often adapting their design processes to facilitate better adaptation to the needs of computer graphics. Systems such as CelAction, for example, have enabled traditional approaches to be adapted to the computer, and more readily supported design strategies that have flat, graphic, compositional qualities drawn from illustration, graphic design and modern art. This has further allowed for the use of often complex, non-Western design idioms, evidenced in recent work by Michel Ocelot.

Ocelot

One of the form's master animators, Frenchman Michel Ocelot, has always been preoccupied with the ways in which technique facilitates persuasive storytelling, and how he as a creative director can find himself in the material. Of *Azur and Asmar* (aka *The Princes' Quest*) (2006) he notes: 'I knew I was going to give six years of my life to a subject. It had to be part of me. So what inhabits me today? All those human beings hating each other and fighting and killing, make me sick. And the few people, in the midst of this ugly madness, who like each other, above the barbed wire, touch me profoundly.... I was to do a fable about being different and about the difficulty of being an immigrant. Immigrants in France are mainly from North Africa, and Muslim. So I added a celebration of this half-forgotten brilliant civilisation of the Middle Ages. I was into a burning subject, but my language is fairy tales, and giving pleasure. So the fable tended towards the *The Thousand and One Nights* aspect, having in mind the aesthetic refinement of Persian miniatures.'

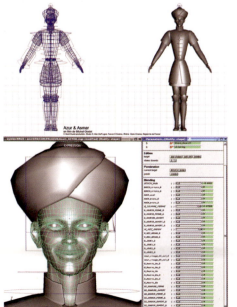

Azur & Asmar
un film de Michel Ocelot

Azur & Asmar
un film de Michel Ocelot

Ocelot felt he could best engage with these visual idioms through a combination of 2D and 3D elements, ensuring that the realisation of the characters and backgrounds would not merely ape the received knowledge and pictorial clichés of the Middle East. The approach also enabled him to experiment: 'I had a few successes recently, and for the new film I could afford a more expensive technique than usual. So I decided to try 3D computer animation, to know new ways and images. This was used for the characters. For the backgrounds, I felt the complication, delay and expense of 3D was not justified. I was not interested in photorealism, and preferred being a painter doing whatever he wants on a flat surface, with greater freedom (even with perspective). This also meant a significant saving of time and money, which is always welcome.'

title
Azur and Asmar

animator
Michel Ocelot

The initial designs for Azur and Asmar reflect particular care in their representation, resisting the clichéd design of the Oriental 'other' that has often characterised Western cartoons, preferring a less caricatured, more realistic depiction. Azur's model sheet shows a colour rendered version of Azur, but uses core drawings to point up his posture, props and interaction with his environment.

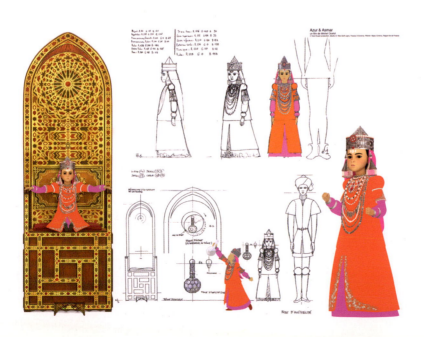

Ocelot underpinned his use of computer-generated animation with drawn approaches. This enabled a greater degree of detail to be added to the designs, and a freedom of expression in the creative development of the film, which would otherwise be inhibited by a need to be in command of the software applications. He stresses: 'All is based on drawing. We took much more time with the hand-drawn preparations than with the actual animation. And the computer people were very happy with what we brought to them; storyboard, model sheets, animatic.'

Indeed, for those seeking to enter the industry it remains insufficient to have high-end technical skills: the ability to animate in a neo-classical style or a hands-on drawn approach is still a key requirement. Often it is the case that 2D work is done by separate hands from 3D animators but, increasingly, and necessarily, these skills must go together. The scale of work done by Ocelot's team in 2D enabled a highly successful facilitation of the 3D work, simply because the information revealed by the drawing enabled the animation to take place. For Ocelot, though: 'The most important part of directing an animated film is the storyboard. I invent my stories and write the dialogue, but it is only when I draw the storyboard that everything takes its final shape, dialogue included. I draw the model sheets of the main characters; a collaborator draws the rest of the cast. All backgrounds are first drawn on paper, then scanned, and coloured; these values and patterns are then created in the computer. I believe the consistent style comes from my being there all the time, and facilitating my collaborators with all the documentation I like, and they require.

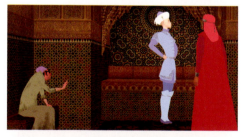

As Ocelot moves through the process, he effectively maintains the style that his original drawings suggest, but also the conceptual premises underpinning the story, which emerged through his drawing: 'Drawing is any thing and any shape and any subject and any movement you want! It is by no means limited to Disney-style animation ('style' is now often replaced by proprietary computer-generated material anyway). It has a simple freedom that computers, slaves to mathematics, perspective, etc, do not have (the main drawback, though, is the tediousness of in-betweens...).'

Ocelot rightly insists that it is the openness of drawing in the first instance that might best enable a resistance to the dominant aesthetics created by 'new traditionalist' animation, or the easy applications of a variety of software programs. Drawing remains the best tool to enable an original approach, challenging the software and its limits, rather than submitting to them. Drawing also properly underpins successful animation, and remains its most pertinent vehicle.

As Ocelot reminds us: 'On one hand, I never try to be a revolutionary, on the other hand, I never thought about doing the same as somebody else. I love the Egyptians, the Greeks (vase paintings), Renaissance (yes, particularly the drawings! Michelangelo, among others), Japan (Hokusai, 'the old man mad with drawing'), Persia, British illustrators from the turn of the century (I mean nineteenth and twentieth), the list is endless, and it grows.'

Azur & Asmar
un film de Michel Ocelot

title
Azur and Asmar

animator
Michel Ocelot

Ocelot's rough drawings give a sense of the nature of the movement, gesture and culture of the characters as they interact. Drawing becomes the most direct indicator of the intended performance, which is readily seen in the final rendered work.

Scenes > **2D to 3D**

Throughout this book, stress has been placed on the versatility of drawing in facilitating the animation process. Drawing is first and foremost a complex tool in expressing a range of ideas and thoughts, but also a procedural action in the development and interrogation of material. Emphasis has been placed on the ways that drawing for animation actually suggests and communicates concepts and emotions through its applications and technique. This chapter explores the ways in which drawing can help facilitate narrative, not merely through the visualisation of storytelling, but through the ways in which the tools at the disposal of the animator, deviser or writer may be used as models of suggestion and experimentation, and readily complement established processes of thinking about generating material.

title
Box improvisation

animator
Kimberley Rice

Animator and tutor Peter Parr underlines the importance of keeping a sketchbook, as follows: 'A sketchbook can be as private or as public as you like. The fact that you have one, and it is tended regularly, allowing you to observe, record, translate, fantasise and have fun, is testament to your commitment. Each mark or scribble you make in your sketchbook, good or bad, goes to make up the important stepping stones that are necessary to the creative process. Don't be tempted to tear pages from your book. A sketch, no matter how slight, should always be kept as it will certainly be used sooner or later. Its primary use to you was its creation. Your sketches will support each other in charting your search.'

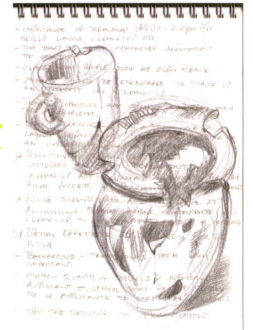

▶▶ Sketchbook drawings

artist
Peter Parr

These sketchbook drawings reveal immediate responses to visual stimuli, attraction to matters of detail and perspective, and comparative models of objects and figures.

This 'search' is especially important because it is not inherently driven by required outcome, but serves to generate important resources that may be used at any time. In the same way that dramatist Mike Leigh, for example, might devise material with his casts, the animator uses drawing as the tool by which matters of record, fantasy and deliberation might be apprehended, providing the inspiration, history and primary ideas for the development of characters, contexts, and cultures.

Parr adds: 'In my sketchbooks I like to try many different drawing tools, from the conventional to the unconventional, and a wide variety of techniques to interpret what I see. I look, think and see before I start to draw. What materials would best suit the subject? Should I try something new? The sketchbook is an important place in which to broaden and preserve your knowledge in your quest to develop your drawing skill. Be receptive in your exploration of nature, art and artists, sculptors or animators in your book: it's your journal of your development as an artist. It provides you with the means to record thoughts and observations to help you build a resource that will inform your work.'

Developing drawing skills

Development of drawing skill is intrinsically bound up with the pursuit of ideas and concepts; 'skill' might imply a particular advancement in technique, but the ability to express graphically as a means to an end – not necessarily to a high standard or in any way finished, except in the sense of 'completed' – is also important. This is in turn related to what the experimental animator Len Lye called 'the bodily stuff' – how expressive feelings emitted through the body find correspondence with the most direct means of their expression through drawing and other physical applications. As Peter Parr argues: 'By my reckoning, if your sketchbook is in your backpack and not in your hand, then it is not with you! It is the act of carrying the book in your hand which prompts your curiosity.'

This remark recognises that, for many, drawing has become a self-conscious, technical act, rather than something that services the immediacy of a felt response. The variety of possible perspectives expressed in a sketchbook, coupled with the playfulness in engaging with ideas, ensures the widest possible vocabulary in creating characters and environments. The personality that underpins the expression will be vital in the creation of fresh material, and engaging ideas.

Parr feels this is crucial: 'My own sketchbooks are a collection of drawings and findings that preserve and interpret my observations, so I can explore and check my skills. They keep me visually alert and technically fit in much the same way as a performer practises or a body-builder builds muscle. If you stop using your sketchbook you run the risk of falling foul of those old demons, uncertainty and self-doubt. Your sketchbook can be a treasury of reference and playfulness which can lead you to discovery and fulfilment in your drawing.' It is important to reiterate that without free expression, drawing skills are not developed and honed and, more importantly, drawing as a vehicle to find meaning and effect in animated film becomes redundant.

Sketches

artist
Peter Parr

Parr engages artistic and material contexts – the work of Rodin, the city of Venice, soccer matches etc – to address issues of scale, detail and perspective, whilst seeking out the vitality and (e)motion in any one image, his chief tools as an animator.

In a similar style to live-action film-maker Mike Leigh, Les Mills and Joanna Quinn seek to devise character in a way that facilitates narrative. By creating a rich backstory and ensuring the character's experiences are seen from a range of perspectives, narrative can emerge through exposition and suggestion, and as dramatic events. This is also enabling in the visualisation process. Quinn's own attempts to use the comic-strip narrative form to develop concise storytelling techniques also illustrate the ways in which visual images can apprehend narrative. As Mills points out: 'The one thing all these comic strips had in common was that the characters were all well observed and beautifully drawn. Joanna was clearly more interested in the mundane realism rather than fantasy. Joanna started to draw comic strips about incidents that happened to her. They were based on reality but exaggerated. However, Joanna was always frustrated with the comic strips because she could never seem to capture the dynamic quality of her heroes.'

In many senses, these frustrations became the prompt to advance Quinn's drawing skills, and her increasing desire to become an animator. Mills and Quinn viewed their representation of the personal conditions of existence as intrinsically political. In Quinn's case, this was concerned with the presence and effect of women creatively and culturally. Mills comments: 'Most of the British independent animation had been male-dominated and generally featured **stereotypical** characters, especially female characters, which were in the main appallingly sexist and docile representations of women – and often fabrications of male fantasies. However, in the late 70s things had begun to change because of the great influence of the feminist movement, Eastern European animation, including work by Jan Svankmajer, and the American and Canadian avant-garde movements in animation and the underground cinema, featuring work by Norman McLaren and Robert Breer.'

title
Girls Night Out

animator
Joanna Quinn

Some early design experiments for Beryl, considering what she would look like facially, how her body might be configured and the kinds of clothes she might wear.

Drawing and narrative

Stereotype characterisation that is informed by only one dominant characteristic, or plays out social attitudes. Animation can both interrogate these typologies and, more often, create more complex characters defined by their interior states.

Developing character

While Quinn learned that narrative could be conceived from a range of different approaches, her real interest was in **character**. Quinn explains: 'It is quite difficult definitively to pinpoint exactly where the character of Beryl came from. I think the character was loosely based on several women I knew. The most obvious was my mother.'

Character the way in which a person acts and behaves, and is spiritually, morally, socially and practically developed through the choices he or she makes.

Mills adds: 'The actual name for the character, Beryl, was chosen because it represented 1940s and 1950s working-class Britain. Other names were considered – Ethel, Elsie, Doris, Mabel, Doreen – but Beryl seemed to fit the part and was finally adopted. Having decided that Beryl was going to become the central character in any narrative, the precise circumstances of Beryl's existence needed to be examined. We had both worked in factories producing a variety of products and the tedium and boredom of conveyor belt existence had a profound effect on us. The realisation that this was what a substantial proportion of the population had to put up with for most of their lives was a salutary lesson.'

In a direct response to the sexism of the times, and the general scepticism about the ultimate success of the feminist movement, Quinn made *Girls Night Out*, a film about Beryl going to a male strip show. Mills notes: 'In the true spirit of research, Joanna actually went to a male striptease night and returned totally shocked by the actual frenzy of the occasion. It was her first real experience of unbridled female lust on a communal scale, and she was quite shocked by the reactions of the women.' This was in many ways even more enabling to Quinn in relation to her drawing, however, in that such events not only underpinned the kind of narrative action that might occur within the film, but this dynamic and passionate emotion contributed to the intrinsic energy of the line.

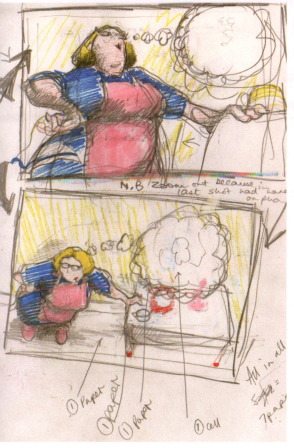

Going out frock

◄◄ ▲

title
Girls Night Out

animator
Joanna Quinn

Quinn starts to dramatise Beryl through her movement in specific situations, even something as ordinary as her sitting on a stool. These brief vignettes of experience become the possible stimuli for narrative development.

Character considerations

This was the beginning of the development of Beryl as a leading anti-heroine that lead directly to *Body Beautiful*, a longer, more tightly scripted film that explored with greater depth the character of Beryl and her workmates and introduced more defined male roles: the infamous Vince, and a more benign and sympathetic husband, Ivor. Mills and Quinn recall: 'The basis for this script was to continue to pursue the idea of an underdog female figure – Beryl – fighting against prejudice and mockery in a predominantly male environment – again, a factory in Wales. We explored many scenarios using sports or games as possible settings – ice hockey, baseball, etc – but we quickly abandoned these ideas because of the complexity of the settings and, of course, the immense task of undertaking the animation itself (huge numbers of moving figures, complex viewpoints, etc). Eventually we decided that if we were going to develop Beryl as a character, we should continue the theme of camaraderie and female unity in the workplace and an unlikely heroine taking on a macho domineering figure on his own terms, and ultimately triumphing. This seemed like a much more manageable proposition and it would give more scope for character development on a more human and intimate scale.'

The narrative- and character-led decisions made by Mills and Quinn were informed by the nature of the drawing required, and the time and resources available. Complex sporting activity, for example, was avoided here, because of the demands of representing the specific kinds of action in sports. To concentrate on this would have ultimately distracted from Beryl and those around her as the core focus of the narrative. As was suggested on page 91, the setting, too, can become a resonant character and suggest narrative possibilities.

Mills notes: 'We decided to reflect this by updating Beryl's work situation from a cake factory [to an electronics factory], specifically the Sony one. Simultaneously we wanted also to reflect issues which Beryl herself as an older, mature woman might be confronting on a daily basis. In this instance it was a weight problem – Beryl's struggle against her expanding body would become the focus of attention, along with her fight against mockery and humiliation by the macho figure of Vince.'

Again, the representation of the body is one of the most fundamental aspects of drawing for animation, but instead of just operating on functional terms and conditions to depict a character, it is used to engage with the subjective experience of the character, too.

The representation of the body…instead of just operating on functional terms and conditions to depict a character, it is used to engage with the subjective experience of the character, too.

Paul Wells

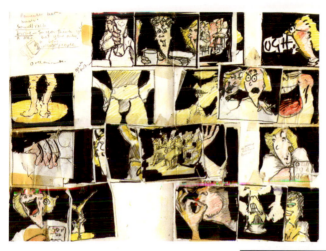

▲

title
Girls Night Out

animator
Joanna Quinn

Quinn moves on from the comic-strip-styled *Girls Night Out* narrative (see page 30) and starts to play with the cinematographic and choreographic potential of her characters and the male strip show.

(see page 30)

Body Beautiful narrative structure

Introduction
Vince, a factory supervisor, is heard extolling his own sexual prowess in relation to the young women in the factory, and abusing Beryl's size and attractiveness. This establishes the core theme of the film, and the central tension between Beryl and Vince.

Realisation
Beryl is encouraged to diet so that she can take part with her colleagues as a dancer in the forthcoming work concert, but struggles.

Beryl's action strategy
Beryl decides to take up a bodybuilding evening class and begins a vigorous training regime. This seeks a resolution to the narrative, while providing significant action towards change.

Climax and resolution
Beryl participates in the 'Body Beautiful' contest and wins.

Sketchbooks as narrative resources > **Character as narrative**

Illustration and narrative

Supinfocom graduates Alexandre Bernard, Pierre Pages and Damien Laurent based the narrative of their film *Marin* (2007) on the specific relationship between a sailor and his pet goldfish. Bernard notes: 'We wanted to direct an original story based on the relationship between the characters with contemplation, action and acting sequences. Everything is based on contrast: the sailor is strong, the fish is tiny and needs water; they are in a world where water has disappeared.'

The team established a colour-coding in their original drawn designs that would underpin the narrative: 'The colours of the film evolve with the story, and we developed a 2D **illustration** technique using a light board. There are three key colours that summarise the film: bright brown for the lifeless and desert environment with no water; blue steel for the underwater sequences, suggesting the return of life; and red for the characters and their hope: the fish, the sailor's T-shirt, the boat and the lighthouse.'

title
Marin

animators
Alexandre Bernard, Pierre Pages and Damien Laurent

The colour-coding in *Marin* narrativises and dramatises the action taking place. Red signifies hope; blue suggests life; brown, barren dystopia.

Illustration the narrative drawing that supports the specific interpretation of a text or concept, predicated on static, graphic principles, which literally interpret or associatively suggest story events and development.

The team's use of colour symbolism and different contexts in which the dramatisation could take place enabled an immediacy in the reading of the images. Illustration is often predicated on a particular stylisation that speaks to this immediacy and which, in this case, also services the approach to computer-generated animation.

▼

Sailor study

animators
Alexandre Bernard, Pierre Pages and Damien Laurent

The main character of the sailor has mythic and everyday qualities to stress both his heroism and his compassion: though the narrative works on an epic scale, its primary message is that in the face of all odds, humankind retains a capacity to love unconditionally and selflessly.

Bernard continues: 'We decided that the sailor should look like a hero of Greek mythology and a 'Papa Bear'. The character's designs are based on stylised and simple shapes with just enough anatomy to animate them; this was helpful to obtain nice silhouettes and also clear and graphic poses. In computer-generated animation characters and environment are built in 3D. We never forgot, however, that the final render would be a flat image and, therefore, the rules of image composition and the striking shapes and silhouettes that can be achieved in animation are the same for 2D and 3D animation. Pre-production is vital in making a computer-generated animated film, because it is made on a computer and by definition it is lifeless, has no artistic sensitivity, and is used only as a tool. We just tried to keep the life and the artistic qualities that were in our 2D concept designs and tried also to match the composition that we established in our storyboard.'

While many argue that the computer is only a tool in the making of a film, Bernard goes further in suggesting that unless the vitality and design sensibility can be readily translated into computer-generated imagery, it may well be an inappropriate tool. To this end, the team's decision to align illustration techniques with animation was highly pertinent in achieving a persuasive outcome. This relates significantly to the team's investment in drawing: 'Drawing is very useful in pre-production; when we build a story there's a lot of round-trip, or revisiting of the intended narrative, and a rough drawing is quick to make and quick to throw away if the idea it illustrates does not serve the story adequately. It is in the storyboard where the action is clearly defined and the intentions of composition are settled in a particular direction and with a specific artistic point of view.'

The *Marin* team made an animatic in parallel to the development of the storyboard, specifically to address the rhythm of the piece and the success of the illustrative approach (see pages 86–89). Again, as Bernard stresses: 'The 2D design process for the characters and the environment is very useful because that is where the graphic unity can be checked. For animation, thumbnailing is a good way to find spontaneous and living poses because it is made in only ten or fifteen seconds instead of searching for a good pose moving a hundred controllers during five or ten minutes on the computer.'

Finding these poses goes back to very traditional approaches to drawing: 'Animation is based on the observation of real life; we think that gesture drawing while watching TV or observing people in the street helps develop an eye for animation. Disney's animators took gesture drawing classes with people such as Walt Stanchfield. That is how they learned not only to draw what they see but to caricature it just enough in the movement to make the drawings more alive, while keeping it credible. If you want to see some of the best drawing for animation, just take a look at some of Glen Keane's animation drawing – it is rough, it is bold and it is alive; we can feel the movement! We don't ignore other styles of drawing for animation, but we feel that our approach to this is closer to Disney's work.'

title
Marin

animators
Alexandre Bernard, Pierre Pages and Damien Laurent

A comparative view of the *Marin* team's animatic – its primary drawings/dramatisation – and the final rendering of the scenes. This fully illustrates the importance of the original drawings in capturing the essential narrative, character relationships and action.

Drawing and narrative

Dance narrative

Norman McLaren was one of the first master animators to emphasise the relationship between dance and animation, arguing that both art forms are predicated predominantly on expression through the conscious act of motion. Anyone attending a ballet or a contemporary dance production recognises narrative in the physical expression of the performers and, though music may well be an aid to the emotional undertow of the piece, it is the nature of bodily movement itself that communicates particular feelings and ideas. In his film *Pas de Deux* (1968), McLaren reanimated a dance sequence by overlaying the images.

Numerous other animators/directors including Monique Renault, Antoinette Starkiewicz, Gianluigi Toccafondo and George Miller have all experimented with dance idioms, but it is Erica Russell who has perhaps forged the closest alliance between the 'bodily stuff' of expressing through drawing and the profound effect of dance itself. In *Feet of Song* (1988), she explored the pure joy and lyricism of dance as personal expression, and in *Triangle* (1994) looked at the passion at the heart of the classic ménage à trois. Her next work, the more challenging *Soma* (2001), was critically less well received.

Soma looks at the body in a different way. Russell is much more concerned with the body as an urban concept: vital yet vulnerable; highly driven yet fragmented and incoherent. This is the body of the break-dance – the dances of the street that echo graffiti-art New Yorker Basquiat's work, and not the dance of theatrical performance. The more jagged, less fluid, attention to the body's limits have about them a modernist spirit, partly casting the body as a machine, but also as an organism prone to possible decay or decline. Intermittent phrases emerge on the screen – 'blood tie', 'body blow', 'back lash', 'leg iron' – suggesting the body in conflict with the environment and itself. This is not the body fused with pleasure, desire and high spirits, but the body in violent turmoil, subject to the arbitrary vicissitudes of the postmodern world. Russell's drawing and painted brushwork ground the body in the everyday and chaotic, resisting the elevated and ethereal escape and the impersonality of the dance. In all her work, though, she captures the very experience of the body through her drawn forms and is expressing her personal vision of motion.

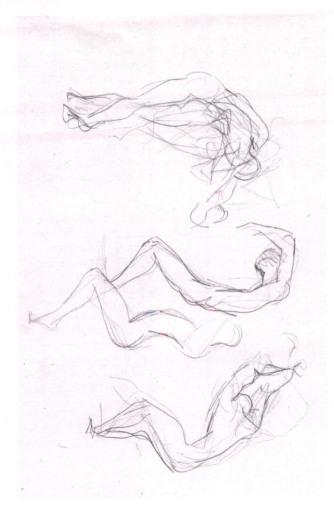

title
Soma

animator
Erica Russell

Russell plays with the modernist conception of the body as a machine, redefining 'soma' as a quasi-industrialised urban organism, its motion subject to new patterns of repetitive, habitual existence that it seeks to resist. The body then begins to show Baconesque qualities of being in tension with itself, operating on a borderline between control and collapse.

Narrative for children

Using drawing as a narrative tool for children's animation is especially important as there is a strong empathetic bond between children's creative practice and animated worlds. These worlds are often drawn – mirroring children's own drawing or illustrations in children's books – or produced in 3D stop-motion animation – resembling the 3D toy environments children play within.

Successful children's animation requires high-quality work and particular skills in storytelling. This kind of work demands a particular versatility and responsiveness to the audience. Curtis Jobling, a writer, illustrator and animator, possesses such versatility and has been open to the challenges in his developing career. Jobling explains: 'I got the call from Jackie Cockle, producer at the newly formed HOT Animation Studios. She was aware of my work and asked me if I'd be interested in designing a new pre-school stop-motion show for them to take to the market. That show was *Bob the Builder*, and it was a blank canvas.'

Though Jobling had to create *Bob the Builder* in three dimensions, the evolution of the character was fundamentally achieved at the design stage: 'My first drawing of Bob that was submitted had to change along the way, but not a great deal. I'd designed him with tiny feet and little hands. This was never going to be practical on a stop-motion puppet show. Our puppets needed to be able to stand firm on the sets and not wobble around and fall over…. So I gave Bob larger feet, which allowed us to fit metal plates beneath them that covered a wide footprint. During animation, magnets were placed under the set located directly beneath the feet to hold Bob and his fellow puppets in place during each shot.'

These points help to stress that when drawing for design purposes, a degree of pragmatism has to underpin the invention. Having some knowledge of how the drawing will be used, or to what applications it must speak, needs to be part of the arsenal of the prospective designer for animation, and necessitates research.

title
Bob the Builder

animator
Curtis Jobling

Jobling's original sketches for the now-iconic Bob the Builder, and his cat, Pilchard. Bob's moustache was later removed as this aged him too much for a children's audience.

Drawing and narrative

The design of Bob dictated how the other
human characters in the show would look.
Working with a generic male and female
puppet that was bald and nude, I simply
had to design wigs and costume designs
for each new character that was introduced
to the show.

Curtis Jobling

One of Jobling's great strengths is his eye for comic caricature and the creation of resonant visual constructs that draw upon other well known pictorial sources and literary tales, themselves rich in illustrative history. Jobling's abilities in illustration are well evidenced in Jon Emmett's book *Dinosaurs after Dark* and in his own story, *Frankenstein's Cat*: 'I used to travel down to London from Warrington frequently, to meet with animation studios, collaborators and publishing houses. On one such trip I set myself the task of creating the basis of a picture book on the two-and-a-bit-hour journey. That's how *Frankenstein's Cat* came into existence. I'd written maybe the first four paragraphs of the story on the journey, and even found time to whip out my pen and do a doodle of how I imagined Nine, Frankenstein's cat, would look. He was called Nine not because cats have nine lives but because that's how many cats it took to make him. He was a patchwork affair, stitched together haphazardly from leftover feline bits, but to me he was instantly recognisable. As a character design on a bumpy train journey down the West Coast Main Line, he was the closest I'd ever come to a character that did exactly what it said on the tin.'

Here it is important to note that Jobling's drawing is working in the service of a core concept drawn from a literary source. Frankenstein's monster in Mary Shelley's novel is a compendium of human parts; it thus follows that Frankenstein's Cat might be constructed in a similar fashion, but in the leavening form of a design strategy.

Jobling's 'multi-coloured doodle' won a commission, and was an obvious candidate for a children's animated series. Interestingly, the drawing/animation itself was key to signalling that Frankenstein's cat is not a real cat – something it was vital to communicate to the young audience – while foregrounding the plausible fantasy of the character, guaranteeing a child would know that Frankenstein's cat is a funny idea. Series such as *Funnybones* and *Grizzly Tales for Gruesome Kids* have worked on similar comic gothic premises, and play on children's attraction to sick jokes and slapstick humour.

title
Frankenstein's Cat

animator
Curtis Jobling

Jobling's original children's story *Frankenstein's Cat*, featuring Nine, a cat patchworked together from the components of nine different cat drawings.

title
Frankenstein's Cat

animator
Curtis Jobling

Jobling's original notebook
sketch for *Frankenstein's Cat*;
a testament in itself to keeping
sketchbooks available and in
use all the time. This was
produced essentially as an
afterthought, but such was the
quality of the idea and the initial
visual conception, its potential
was recognised immediately.

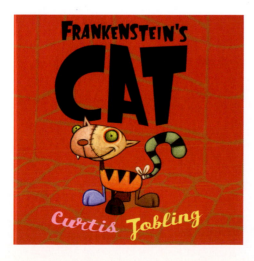

Jobling was keen to work with Mackinnon & Saunders, with whom he had also worked on *Curious Cow*, as they sought to become an independent production company, so he pitched *Frankenstein's Cat* to them. His designs were pertinent to the technology that could produce them, and economically viable as a consequence. More importantly, Jobling retained a pragmatic signature style: 'The actual design of Nine only changed slightly from the book to the TV show. You'll recognise the trademark big, clumpy feet, which appear on a lot of my characters. The change came in the tail – wanting to make our cat even more distinctive from other feline animated characters that already existed, I ditched the stripy, slinky, quizzical tail for a broken-looking, crank-handled, spotty affair. The colour, green, remained the same. As we developed the story structure we realised that Nine needed a friend. That's where Lottie enters the frame.'

Jobling's stress on story and the centrality of character should not be undervalued, but the visualisation of the piece is fundamental to potential appeal and, ultimately, successful merchandising. However, many children's stories inevitably feature a main character and their pet – William and Barksure, Postman Pat and his black-and-white cat, the boy and his pet cat in the *Charley Says* 1970s public information campaign and, most famously, Wallace and Gromit. Frankenstein's cat is ultimately joined by Lottie: 'Lottie, as it happens, is the only girl in the village of Oddsburg, sticking out like a sore thumb in a classroom full of boys. The boys don't let her join in any of their games even though we all know she's smarter, faster, stronger and better all-round than the narrow-minded boys. Back at the castle, Nine finds himself alone as well, surrounded by Frankenpets who pick on him all the time. Lottie and Nine meet and their friendship is at the heart of the show. They don't fit in, but they fit together.'

title
Curious Cow

animator
Curtis Jobling

Jobling's character design and sight gags for the mad heifer, *Curious Cow*, first animated in 3D stop-motion by Mackinnon & Saunders, then in 3D CGI by Seed Animation.

Rarely is a design immediately accepted, with redrawing to address certain constituencies of viewer or issues of inappropriate interpretation commonplace. Jobling explains: 'Of all the characters I've designed for animation, Lottie has been through the most permutations, as we looked to settle on something appropriate. The first design I did of her had big bunches in her hair, and she looked altogether a bit young, something broadcasters were picking up on. To age her up and contemporise her we gave her stripy leggings, baseball boots, and took her for a makeover to the cartoon hair salon. It was going to be no good giving her a look that was going to date, and that was the challenge. The rest of the cast are as stupid looking as we could get away with, pushing extremities as far as was possible'.

title
Frankenstein's Cat

animator
Curtis Jobling

Lottie becomes an intrinsic part of the narrative: she teams up with Nine, another outsider, and together they resist the torments and teasing of their adversaries.

Adaptation – the process of animating images using someone else's established drawing or graphic style – has become an important aspect of professional animation drawing, with ever more comics, graphic novels and illustrations being transformed into animated form. Because the original source material is often in drawn form, the process of adaptation is one of re-presentation, preserving the integrity of the stylistic characteristics of the work, while finding ways to animate it.

This can be problematic on a number of levels. Raymond Briggs's work for children's books, for example, has a strong impressionistic pastel styling that is time-consuming to animate, although this has been achieved impressively by TVC London in productions such as *The Snowman* (1982), *When the Wind Blows* (1986) and *Father Christmas* (1991). Heinz Edelmann's graphic design for *Yellow Submarine* (1968), however, was so problematic to animate, with its uses of stripes, surreal flat planes and over-decorated designs, that the distinctiveness of the piece has rarely been copied, and it has not proved as influential as its achievement would seem to warrant.

◄

title
NBC advertisement

artist
**Al Hirschfield /
JJ Sedelmaier**

JJ Sedelmaier Productions work in a number of styles for a range of clients, and are often required to animate a well-known illustrator or drawing stylist's work. Sedelmaier himself notes: 'First off, my role in all this is as a director/art director. I often choose not only the graphic artist responsible for designing the look of the animation, but also gather together my animation crew based on the talents of the individual artists. It is useful to think of an animator as the actor and the assistant artists as supporting actors. Even though a good animator can work in a variety of styles and sensibilities, they also have realms of performance that they can really sparkle in. I try to cast the crew based on these strengths.

'Each and every instance of translating art from print to film is different – ideally, it HAS to be! Each artist's style has its own unique qualities that steer the choice of movement, rendering and even sound design.'

Yellow Pages advertisement

animator
George Booth and
JJ Sedelmaier

The initial brief for this advert required an illustration with a simple line style on a yellow background characteristic to the product. Although Booth's animation work demonstrated the necessary quality of line, it was peopled with elderly Middle-American eccentrics with a WC Fields-style sense of humour. As soon as Booth was committed to the project, however, the brief was revised to accommodate his characters and scenarios.

Drawing and adaptation

◀

Home Savings Bank advertisement

animator
JJ Sedelmaier

Sedelmaier's ad for the Home Savings Bank deliberately adapts the modernist cartoon styling of UPA from the mid 1950s, suggesting the progressive work of Stephen Bosustow, Dave Hilberman, Zack Schwartz and John Hubley, while recalling the reassurance of the 1950s for contemporary savers.

Maintaining aesthetic stylings

There are a number of reasons why retaining the integrity of an established graphic or illustration style in animation is important:

To sustain its authenticity in a different medium.

To reach new audiences and potential customers who are already familiar with the original work of the author.

To sustain a style that has become distinctive in a print medium, so it too becomes original and affecting.

To maintain an authorial point of view, or a particular tone; for example, the satirical charge of political cartooning.

To capitalise on the iconic value of the original styling, thereby adding to the animation's meaning and effect.

There are a number of issues involved in moving from a static, single image to creating an animated commercial. These vary from project to project, but in general, as Sedelmaier stresses: 'The director and the animator have to make it appear as though the artist has animated their own work! They have to thoroughly understand how the artist/designer communicates with their audience in order to successfully translate that technique into another realm – animation. More often than not, this involves developing animation techniques that are original to the project.'

He adds: 'The animation team also needs to be aware of any "baggage" that is associated with the artist's work. For instance, if an artist with a recognisable style and a reputation for biting political satire has been chosen for a particular project, the film-maker needs to be aware that the audience could be bringing preconceived notions to the viewing.'

Sedelmaier is particularly adept at models of adaptation because he refutes any particular signature style of his own, preferring to work in a number of styles and in a variety of roles: 'I don't think of myself as having a "style"…if you look at the projects in both print and animation that I've designed, you'll find quite a variety of graphic approaches. I really enjoy hiding within the design or developing styles, and with so much of our work dwelling in the world of parody and satire, it's helped to be chameleon-like in terms of graphic design.'

Drawing analysis

In any project there has to be a 'drawing analysis' of the original artist/illustrator's style and how it fits into the project as a whole. Sedelmaier lists here the significant areas for consideration:

Identify the technique that defines the artist's work (eg watercolour, pen and ink, marker, PhotoShop, Illustrator).

Does the sensibility of the artist's storytelling approach match with the artwork (eg is it satirical, biting, gentle, humorous?).

From these first two phases both the sequential movement of the characters and the movement of the rendering technique can be determined – for instance, how much should the watercolour texture 'flutter' or 'boil'?

Finally, the sound design must imbue the animation with the appropriate attitude; the wrong sound design will make a beautiful piece of animation fall flat.

title
Charmin advertisements

animator
Joanna Quinn

Quinn employed a more cartoon-like style for the Charmin commercial narratives, but they still retain a gentle British flavour echoing the early post-war *Animaland* cartoons made by Gaumont British Animation.

Drawing and adaptation

Adapting a signature style

While Sedelmaier's task was to animate the illustration and graphic design styling of others, Joanna Quinn adapted her signature-style drawing for commercials for Charmin toilet rolls, which necessitated that she maintain an integrity of approach in the design of the now-iconic Charmin bear. She explains: 'The starting point for me always when animating an animal is to draw from life, ie visit the zoo, watch wildlife documentaries and compile photographic reference. So my first character sheets are always realistic interpretations, so I can try to identify what makes a bear, ie his weight, back of neck, snout, eyes, the way he walks.... My first character sheet was sent to the agency, who identified what they thought were the important visual characteristics that they wanted to see accentuated in the Charmin bear. Personality-wise they wanted the bear to be reliable, down to earth, friendly, cuddly...a sort of gentle giant.

'Armed with their comments I went away and did some more sketches which were less realistic and more exaggerated and simplified. The agency commented and I did more, changing and refining each time. I probably sent about five sheets of bears until they were happy. It was quite hard and probably took a couple of weeks. When I see the Charmin ads on television all I can see is myself in the bear, so I instantly sit up straight and stop slouching. Ggrrrrrr.'

Literary adaptation and graphic narrative

Tim Fernée entered animation via the Richard Williams Studio and worked on commercials and shorts for some years. His particular focus has been in literary adaptation, drawing upon the narrative events and descriptive aspects of a language-based text and presenting it through the highly condensed and suggestive language of animation. He won Ireland's first BAFTA for Best Children's Animation for *Sir Gawain and the Green Knight* (2002), which successfully took a well known, if arcane, story, and contemporised it for modern audiences, its heroic action idioms proving to be appealing elements for younger audiences versed in cinematic composition, spectacle and conflict. *Rowlandson Rides Again* (1999) works similarly, while Fernée's web animations as part of a German initiative to bring its fairy tale heritage to a new audience seek to re-historicise increasingly non-literary viewers with influential stories from the past. He has developed *Melmoth the Wanderer* (the first of the great Irish Gothic novels) as a feature film and graphic novel.

Comparing key features

Graphic novel

▶ Frame/panel format (varying dimensions and shapes in depicting single image).

▶ Static sequential narrative.

▶ Framing devices (to show passage of time/movement).

▶ Lettering (context and dialogue).

▶ Visual style.

▶ Conventions (cropping, staging, sound effects, speech bubbles, etc).

Drawing and adaptation

Animated cartoon

▶ Mise-en-scène (compositional choices/ choreographed motion).

▶ Moving sequential narrative.

▶ Metamorphosis/ condensation/symbolic association.

▶ Dialogue/descriptive material presented visually.

▶ Aesthetic choices.

▶ Layout/soundtrack/ referencing conventions (placing recognisable visual signs, etc in motion).

Fernée responds to the dual contexts of the graphic novel and the animated cartoon with different styles of drawing, engaging with all the conventions for drawing that have emerged in both forms. While both are essentially about visualisation, their supporting conventions – the language available through which narrative might be expressed – determine how the act of drawing itself might depict the idea or concept. In all of Fernée's work, he is taking such established visual codes and stylings – whether they are from fine-art sources or graphic- or interior-design idioms – and adapting them for animation, but for an audience, and their awareness or expectation of certain forms. These kinds of adaptation merely highlight the embeddedness of drawing in the **sign** systems that have emerged to visualise cultural forms, and which Fernée, and other animators in this chapter, are highly sensitive to.

◀

title
King of the Birds

animator
Tim Fernée

Fernée advises: 'Drawing informs the simplest production process of all – here represented by a hand-rendered production still from *King of the Birds* (1996).'

Sign a visual signifier of specific social and cultural information and/or meaning; much is made of the role of signs in semiotic analysis.

Fernée has a strong sense of how drawing can carry the mood and atmosphere of a literary text, and how characters essentially develop the story. This informs his animation and graphic narrative, creating immediacy through visual motifs, symbols and dramatic staging. Fernée trusts the visual literacy of his audience because he recognises that in many senses animation operates as a 'hard copy' of a particular felt experience and an intuitive technical skill, and that in producing a memory he has a direct connection with an audience's recognition and empathy.

The images, right, are from Fernée's current adaptation project, *Melmoth the Wanderer*, which was also previously developed by Fernée as a graphic novel.

▲ ▼

title
Sir Gawain and the Green Knight

animator
Tim Fernée

A preliminary line drawing using biro and felt tip, and the finished digipainted production still, evoking the imagery of stained glass to set the film firmly in the medieval period.

title
Melmoth the Wanderer

animator
Tim Fernée

Storyboard undergoing parallel development as graphic novel (light pencil).

Storyboard page sketched quickly in biro and scanned using PhotoShop into hard copy and animatic.

Fernée trusts the visual literacy of his audience because he recognises that in many senses animation operates as a 'hard copy' of a particular felt experience and an intuitive technical skill, and that in producing a memory he has a direct connection with an audience's recognition and empathy.

Paul Wells

Commercials > Literary adaptation and graphic narrative > Adapting aesthetics

Using graphic conventions

Graphic conventions begin as tools by which particular kinds of visualisation and recognition are achieved. Such conventions emerge over time and become the rules that both determine how something is specifically achieved, and how it might ultimately be challenged and progressed. The rise of the web has further bridged the gap between drawing and its animation and has led not merely to progressive work, but to a reclamation, revision and representation of recognisable forms. Comics have always shared a parallel history with animation and, in the first instance, many of the conventions cited above that characterise graphic narratives such as comics appeared in animated cartoons. Speech bubbles emerged in *Felix the Cat* cartoons, for example, but where such a convention was obviously a steal from 'the funnies', the graphic manipulation and metamorphosis also present in the films was animation's distinctive contribution. It has always been the case that comics, graphic narratives and animation have shared a bond, and with that a playful self-reflexive use of their established codes and conventions.

This continues in the present time with work, for example, by Let Me Feel Your Finger First, who wish to foreground their interfaces. The Let Me Feel Your Finger First collective (LMFYFF) trained at art schools in London in the 1990s. LMFYFF explain: 'The first LMFYFF comics feature quite "blocked" bad drawings as the style was only just starting to emerge. The first LMFYFF animation, *Homo Zombies* (2003), came from the idea to animate a story from one of the comics and the approach was to try and bring the drawings to life in a very simple way. So we did redesign and simplify the characters somewhat from the drawings in the comics, but without destroying all the detail in the characters.

▶

title
Francis

animator
Let Me Feel Your Finger First

Francis is initially characterised by a sense of inertia, essentially only animated by the unseen presence of the animator, the psychotherapist voice-over, or the attentions of the implied audience.

'It was at this stage that the LMFYFF style started to take shape (ie the width of the outline became consistent and all the characters developed freckles on their cheeks!). The animation, though, was deliberately clunky and minimal; we'd animate features or specific parts of the characters, rather than redrawing each frame in traditional animation style. Actually, when we made *Homo Zombies* we had no idea how to animate in the traditional Disney way and animated the drawings in quite a haphazard manner.

'With *Francis* (still in production) we continued working in this rather undisciplined way but had decided to employ a professional character animator (Elroy Simmons) to animate the sections where Francis appears to be transforming into a 'real' cartoon character. So I learnt more about traditional animation techniques, about dope sheets etc, through working with a professional. But drawing for animation for LMFYFF continues to be an exploratory process.'

▶

title
Francis

animator
Let Me Feel Your Finger First

Francis's vocal expressions are visualised in the style of traditional comics, but are challenging points of expression, not directed at a specific person or audience.

In specialising in web delivery, and prioritising the creation of online comics and animation, LMFYFF remain experimental both in the use of drawing and the ways in which a vision is finally apprehended: 'It is a mixture of different techniques – a lot of it is intuitive, but at times I'll draw from observation; a lot of the time we'll use visual reference material (photographs, video of movements, etc) and refer back to earlier drawings. For *Francis* we had a nine-year-old model who acted out a lot of the movements as reference. And we embrace repetition! But a lot of it is working out the animation through the drawing, trying something out, deciding it doesn't work, binning it and starting again.

'In terms of an overview of the process used in *Francis*, usually there were rough drawings in pencil of the first and last frames of a sequence, followed by in-betweens, then ink versions, which were then scanned, coloured in Photoshop, and animated in After Effects.'

LMFYFF have currently only worked in 2D, but have a clear recognition that drawing for animation carries with it a metaphysical charge, and suggests the condensation and distillation of a set of complex ideas, even in its most apparently innocent forms. Their Animate-commissioned film *Francis* explores this idea. LMFYFF explain: 'We are interested in the idea of animation and in how this process seems in many ways analogous to our own experience of existence. So I'm interested in what it means to be "animated" and what might constitute "animated behaviour". The "defective child" suggested to us a character who is not working properly in some way or who is somewhere between animate and inanimate. That in itself is interesting to me – something not working properly – so the conventions and codes used refer to accepted ideas about the way animation works and the way characters should behave. And I suppose point out how odd some of those conventions are.'

KEYFRAME!

LMFYFF deliberately use established comic-book and animation conventions to suggest that these very mechanisms work as the controlling agents to particular models of existence and expression. LMFYFF note: 'The presence of the animator's hand in the frame is obviously the first convention that *Francis* uses. This one goes right back to the beginning of animation with J Stuart Blackton's *Humorous Phases of Funny Faces* (1906), and regularly appears in Fleischer Brothers and Looney Tunes work. We are interested in the all-powerful creator who can enhance, transform or erase his creation.'

LMFYFF continue: 'The sequence where Francis has an outburst of cartoon tics refers to the oddball mannerisms so often found in animated characters (Bugs Bunny's incessant chewing, Woody Woodpecker's laugh, Roadrunner's beep, Porky Pig's stuttering, Mutley's dry laugh, etc) and might suggest that he is breaking out and becoming more of an animated character. His blurting out of "Keyframe!" perhaps indicates that he's somehow trying to take control of his animated world.'

title
Francis

animator
Let Me Feel Your Finger First

LMFYFF play with comic book and animation conventions to point up the very difference that they ultimately represent, signalling interior states and external coercion.

LMFYFF explain:

'The psychologist talks about Francis in a kind of hybrid language that includes technical terms referring to animation defects ("he's not frame-accurate", "might suffer from jitter", "overlap", etc). The spinning vortex that Francis disappears into at the end of the film is another cartoon convention, most obviously associated with the Tasmanian Devil. And then there's Pinocchio, the original simple boy trying to break out, but being led astray.'

Francis is a challenging film because of its juxtaposed image of the dysfunctional boy and the psychobabble rhetoric that seeks to define, manage and control him: 'Francis is a hybrid work, and the voice-over reflects this; the narrator is actually a former child-psychologist so the voice-over includes some of his observations. Then there's also the animation terminology. The large part of it though is the language of the 1960s psychologist formulating opinions about the "retarded" child, language that can be very harsh but sometimes also very suggestive. It is also a language that often reveals more about the context of the speaker than the child.

I think of Francis as a film about animation and about animate or maybe inanimate behaviour. It is playful and it celebrates animation, but it pokes a finger at the motivations behind Disney's sugar-coated simpletons as well.

Let Me Feel Your Finger First

'I did a lot of research for another project into the invention of "feeblemindedness" in Victorian England and you come across these incredible and absurd differentiations (moral idiot, idio-imbecile, lower-grade and higher-grade types, etc) that seem to have been formulated by scientists, philanthropists and others seeking to justify controlling and incarcerating children and youths who appeared to be "not normal". At points during the animation it seems unclear whether the psychologist is interpreting Francis's behaviour or instigating it through his descriptions, and Francis certainly starts to resist the psychologist as the assessment progresses.'

LMFYFF has embraced drawing not merely as a tool of expression but as a set of codes that fix certain things, and require challenge. *Francis* seems to be fundamentally about this: 'I think of *Francis* as a film about animation and about animate or maybe inanimate behaviour. It is playful and it celebrates animation, but it pokes a finger at the motivations behind Disney's sugar-coated simpletons as well.'

title
Francis

animator
Let Me Feel Your Finger First

Francis begins to resist both the control of the animator and the controlling counselling of the psychologist.

Commercials > Literary adaptation and graphic narrative > Adapting aesthetics

Adapting comic book sources

Mike Mignola's extremely popular *Hellboy* graphic narratives have found yet further success in the live-action film adaptations directed by Guillermo del Toro (starring Ron Perlman as the mutated devil figure), and later their adaptation into animated form by Tad Stones at Revolution Studios. Intrinsic to this success was Sean 'Cheeks' Galloway's distinctive approach in adapting Mignola's iconic graphic designs and storytelling techniques in the animated Hellboy films *Sword of Storms* (2006) and *Blood and Iron* (2007).

In the animated version, Mignola's signature placing of characters high in the frame so that the viewer seems to be looking up at them, and employing rapid shifts in perspective, were seamlessly re-presented in the animation, while trademark uses of colour to enhance mood and atmosphere were also readily embraced in the more exaggerated effects. For the most part, the animated version resists Mignola's off-centre framing in preference to an almost continual sense of motion and, crucially, the rethinking of character design to facilitate the requirements of animation.

In *Hellboy*, Galloway had not only to work with an iconic character, but also to resolve particular problems that the character presented such as not being symmetrical, with his 'right hand of doom' and, further, in making sure that backgrounds, layouts, other characters and effects complemented his red body colour. Galloway's main achievement was to soften Mignola's original design, rounding out the character and reinventing him as a shape in the first instance, one that worked in silhouette and offered a particular bounce and energy in its construction. Crucially, this design enabled Hellboy to be configured in the standard five-point construction required for this kind of animation, which is based on a 360-degree turnaround.

Galloway's redrawing of Hellboy rendered him a 3D sculptural figure that could readily exist in full graphic environments and facilitate the action required of the character in more heightened fantastical situations and narratives. Mignola's vertical stacking of graphic images was replaced by a 3D depth of field and continual movement. This highly persuasive adaptation has enabled Hellboy to exist afresh in a number of cross-platform environments where each one can add to the iconography and narrative development of the character, rather than merely copying another.

▲

title
**Hellboy Animated:
Sword of Storms**

director
Phil Weinstein

Hellboy finds himself in a
samurai-styled adventure in his
first animated film. The art
direction is based on a number
of Japanese design idioms,
echoing the popularity of manga
and anime with Western
audiences, and the success of
Genndy Tartakovsky's *Samurai
Jack* TV series.

Five-point construction

In order for a figure to be animated
convincingly with full recourse to
cinematic staging, all angles of the
character must be considered and drawn.
Most model sheets emphasise these key
five points, and often add many other
perspectives and points of detail.

1. Full front perspective.

2. Three-quarter front perspective.

3. Profile.

4. Three-quarter back perspective.

5. Side(s).

For example see page 96.

Adapting aesthetics

Nina Paley is a gifted artist and animator whose film, *Sita Sings the Blues* (2008), successfully draws upon complex graphic idioms to create a different kind of feature aesthetic from the Hollywood model. It also reflects the independent and original spirit that characterised Paley's development as an artist in her formative years. Paley reflects: 'All kids draw, but I never lost interest in it. Art is a joy. I consider myself self-taught. My high school offered no art classes, which was good – if they had rammed art down my throat, I would have grown to hate it as much as my other subjects. Drawing to me was always outside of what I was supposed to be doing, free from obligation and drudgery, unlike school. After I left school I could really learn. For many years I really resented how school sucked the time and energy I could have been using to learn, had I been on my own.'

Paley remains constantly surprised that the same issues are repeatedly raised about the animated form, namely that it is predominantly for children, and that it is not really 'art'. She ripostes: 'It is just drawing. You can animate anything, any style. Haven't the last 40 years of independent animation gotten through to people?'

title
Sita Sings the Blues

animator
Nina Paley

Paley's work employs design idioms specific to the project, here using the more formal 2D flat compositions of Indian miniature painting to illustrate her depiction of the *Ramayana*.

Sita Sings the Blues

This sense of independence informs Paley's own distinctive approach: 'Sometimes things just pop into my head and I jot them down in a little notebook as crude sketches, to be refined later. If I'm working on a film, the drawings serve a story or message. The message guides the art – I hardly think about it, I just let the story tell me what is needed. When I wanted to evoke the more stilted, old-fashioned retelling of the *Ramayana*, I tried to imitate Indian miniature painting. I bought natural antique-pigmented watercolours and unbleached brown parchment. I'm not a very good painter, but the materials and technique were enough to convey my intentions.'

She continues: 'For the semi-autobiographical segments, I wanted a scribbly style reminiscent of the picture journals I kept at the time. These I did freehand, using Flash and my beloved Cintiq monitor. I just drew straight in, without any clean-ups. It gives everything a nice raw angsty effect.'

▶

title
Sita Sings the Blues

animator
Nina Paley

Paley plays out her own story in a more personal drawing style, which is both cartoonish and authorial.

Sita Sings the Blues, as its title suggests, incorporates songs, but again, there is a resistance to the 'production number' sensibility of many of the romantic animated features produced, for example, at Disney in the 1990s. Paley prioritised an aesthetic response to the songs above their staging: 'The musical numbers employ a smooth colorful style I developed in 2002, when I was living in Trivandrum. The visuals were surely influenced by the Indian art I saw all around me, as well as the modern Western and Japanese cartoon art popular with the young animators I met there. I sketched the first character designs on paper, then I redid them as 2D puppets in Flash, using smooth strokes and flat colours. I also made some scenes with collage and vector-based shadow puppets. I did a few preliminary pencil sketches for these, but mostly they involved masking photographs and found images.'

Of *Sita Sings the Blues*, Paley remarks: 'I didn't do that much drawing. I'd make sketches in the initial process of character design, then polish things in Flash. I didn't do much storyboarding either, just the occasional scribbly notes if I was having trouble working out a scene. Sometimes the mere act of drawing gets the mind moving to solve problems. There was no typical storyboard for *Sita Sings the Blues*, although there was one for the song "Am I Blue".'

title
Sita Sings the Blues

animator
Nina Paley

Paley's composited images suggest an artisanal collage approach even when employing contemporary animation software applications.

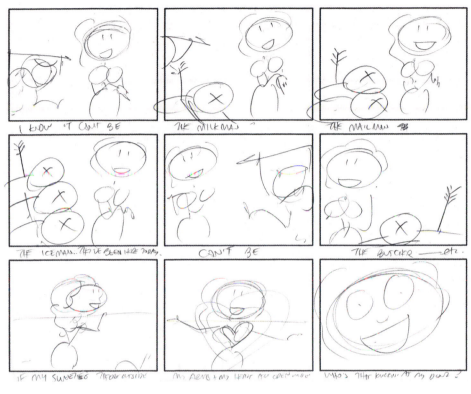

title
Sita Sings the Blues

animator
Nina Paley

Paley's storyboards are often
basic sketches and drawn
improvisations that enable her to
solve narrative or compositional
difficulties she encounters in her
own practice.

Literary adaptation and graphic narrative > Adapting aesthetics

Female sage

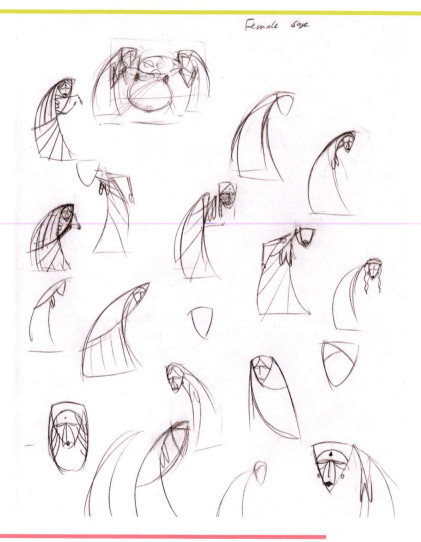

Drawing is an aid to thinking. It's a way to work out ideas, just like writing an outline or notes. It doesn't matter what these sketches look like, just as it doesn't matter what your handwriting looks like when you're making notes.

Nina Paley

Drawing and adaptation

Although this discussion has stressed how important a storyboarding process can be, individual artists inevitably work within their own style, and use drawing where it best aids their practice. Paley comments: 'Most scenes weren't boarded at all. Because I worked alone, the board didn't have to communicate the film to anyone else. They were just a way for me to work out ideas, not present them. However, there were character sketches for the female sages I call Rishettes. I don't have a lot of pre-production art to show for *Sita*, but I did a lot of thumbnail sketches on scraps of paper and little notebooks.'

title
Sita Sings the Blues

animator
Nina Paley

Paley's original sketch conception of a Rishette and the final image in the film. The sketch works as a minimal notation towards the final design, but is helpful in terms of the shape and form of the eventual character.

Literary adaptation and graphic narrative > **Adapting aesthetics**

This chapter features case studies from a range of artists at varying stages in their careers who have engaged with drawing in a distinctive way, and created work that exemplifies many of the characteristics of the approach discussed throughout this book. All have established themselves as exemplars of particular ways of using drawing, and their work is evidence of the act of thinking through drawing for conceptual as well as aesthetic ends. Crucial to all the artists here is the way in which their drawing enables them to facilitate a highly personal vision, often informed by an ideological or artistic agenda, bringing politics to art and art to politics and, further, particular challenge to any accepted orthodoxies of what drawing for animation is, and what it might be used for. In this, the artists often have recourse to outsider forms that challenge social, cultural or aesthetic norms, and also focus attention to the way in which animated drawing captures particular kinds of memory or felt experience. Their drawing is used for formalist yet highly empathetic statements, and while recalling all the conventions of quality animated draughtsmanship, subvert, revise and personalise to singular visions and views.

title
2D or Not 2D

animator
Paul Driessen

Frédéric Back is one of the acknowledged masters of animation, with a distinctive style and approach that marks out his status as one of the form's true **auteurs**. His films are characterised by a highly detailed mise-en-scène, in which the extraordinary quality of the draughtmanship creates a unique aesthetic reminiscent of Impressionist painting.

Back explains: 'It was in making *All Nothing* (1978) that I found "my" technique, when I tried drawing with coloured pencil on frosted cels, a material more commonly used by architects and engineers. This allowed me to reduce the size of the drawings and to use coloured pencil, which wouldn't have adhered to the smooth surface of a transparent cel. The semi-transparency of the frosted cel gives a certain texture to the image and enables great freedom of expression. Wax-based coloured pencils (I used Prismacolor) came in a wide range of colours and were readily available. I gradually perfected the technique and re-used it in my subsequent films.'

Back recognised that his drawing embodied a specific 'material' sense that suggested a certain degree of physical tactility as much as the execution of the line for its own sake. By using frosted cels, Back could combine drawings, add pastel for denser shading in the image, and apply paint on the reverse side of the cel for further effect. This method often involved working with a magnifying glass, and presented further obstacles: 'The problem was that the manufacturers who produced these cels…began to make the frosted side smoother. This meant that the pigments no longer adhered as well as they did to the older, grainier cels…. I had great difficulty making *The Mighty River* (1993) with this newer and less interesting cel, on which the colours appeared less vivid and the line less vigorous.'

Drawing characters and concepts

Auteur auteur theory was espoused during the 1950s and promoted the view of the film director as the sole author of a film, and as a figure with consistent thematic and aesthetic concerns across a body of work. It can be pertinently applied to animation film-makers who often create the whole work themselves.

title
The Man Who Planted Trees

animator
Frédéric Back

Back's more developed
storyboards with images
similar to those actually drawn
for the film.

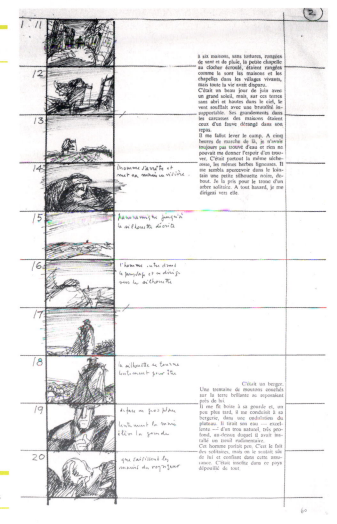

title
The Man Who Planted Trees

animator
Frédéric Back

Back's original planning for *The
Man Who Planted Trees*.

Back has been especially revered for the scale of personal effort and investment he brings to his films. Working outside of Disney's classical model of production, Back completed the detail of the 2D animated sequences himself, rather than using teams of 'in-betweeners'. This approach ensured that his unique aesthetic – which draws upon fine art sources – characterised the films. Although Back's larger-scale projects did ultimately require assistants, their efforts were still overseen and sometimes redrawn by Back himself to ensure homogeneity of style. Of his influences, Back notes: 'The allusions I try to evoke in my films are my way of reaching out to viewers so that they feel on familiar ground and are more receptive to the ideas contained in the images. And so you have references to the Altamira and Lascaux cave paintings in *All Nothing* or to the Impressionists in *The Man Who Planted Trees* (1987).'

Though Back's films have a uniform quality, his masterpiece is, arguably, *The Man Who Planted Trees*, the extraordinary tale (adapted from the story by Jean Giono) of one man's endeavour to repopulate miles of barren plains with trees. It is a narrative that echoes Back's endeavours, as it required him to draw thousands of images to create an emotive and impassioned ecological message to new audiences in the era of global warming. *The Man Who Planted Trees* also represents the ways in which Back's accumulative drawing style mirrors the sense of evolution and development within the narrative itself. Giono's story is wholly respected by Back, whose animation employs a solemn, realistic idiom, recognising the resonance and impact of animation as a form.

Drawing characters and concepts

The visual interest of a pencil drawing is as much a question of texture as it is of method. Covering large surfaces with coloured pencil did not yield interesting animated effects. I decided to work small as much as possible, ideally within a 10×15 cm frame. During projection, the resulting enlargement of the pencil marks gave character to the line and colour.

Frédéric Back

title
The Man Who Planted Trees

animator
Frédéric Back

Back's extraordinary achievement in drawing is reflected in the extraordinary achievement of the man planting trees in the narrative. For Back, animation is not just an art form, but a spiritual vocation dedicated to expressing important ideas and feelings about the human condition and the natural environment.

Frédéric Back > Paul Driessen

Dutch master animator Paul Driessen has always approached his films in a way that is not merely about storytelling but also the formalist challenge he gives himself in the construction of the piece. Ultimately, these are all drawing challenges, and serve to delineate both the distinctive character of his films and points that aspiring animators/ draughtspersons can learn from. Reflecting on Driessen's work enables the viewer to recognise how placing restrictions upon, or testing hypotheses through, drawing stimulates narrative and conceptual development in any one piece.

▶

title
Air!

animator
Paul Driessen

Air! is one of the first examples of Driessen using 'the line' to test the formal properties of the screen. A line bisects the frame and becomes a landscape, the surface of the sea, a telegraph line and a path, each the touchstone for the realisation that there is insufficient air for plants, fish, birds and humankind, as it slowly but surely pollutes its world.

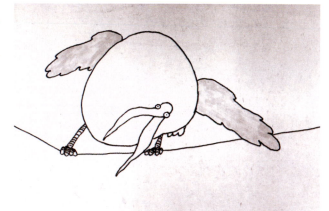

▲

title
Cat's Cradle

animator
Paul Driessen

In *Air!*, Driessen uses the drawn line to point up contexts and concepts. In *Cat's Cradle*, he uses the line to prompt associations, using the likeness between the well-known game played by pulling lengths of string into shapes between fingers, and a spider's web, to drive an intriguing and, ultimately, surreal narrative, in which a 'holy' family are pursued by warriors, and a fish devours all it encounters!

Frédéric Back > **Paul Driessen** > Richard Reeves

▶

title
**On Land, At Sea and In the
Air; The End of the World in
Four Seasons**

animator
Paul Driessen

In his films, *Sunny Side Up*
(1985) and *Tip Top* (1984),
Driessen animated one half of
the screen and merely reversed
it for the bottom half, playing
with the conventions of
symmetry, modifying the idea
again in *The Waterpeople*
(1991). This deliberate
challenging of drawing
conventions and use of the
frame advances a different
model of animated storytelling.

Driessen takes this 'split-
screening' further by having
three parallel screens in *On
Land, At Sea and in the Air*
(1980) and eight separate
frames in *The End of the World
in Four Seasons* (1995).
Driessen uses multiple frames to
play with parallel narratives, to
contrast depictions of action
from afar, in close-up and from
different angles etc, but most
often to draw attention to the
illusionism of drawing in creating
narrative, and as a pure graphic
idiom for its own sake.

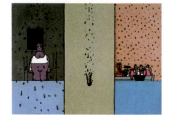

Drawing characters and concepts

title
The Boy Who Saw the Iceberg

animator
Paul Driessen

The Boy Who Saw the Iceberg (2000) shows Driessen using split-screen technique again, employing colour and black and white to differentiate between the real world and a child's parallel fantasy existence. The latter is characterised by 'Boy's Own Adventures' full of spectacle and intrigue, set against the often static routines of domestic life.

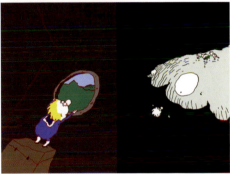

title
2D or Not 2D

animator
Paul Driessen

In the contemporary era 3D animation dominates the medium and this is often used to suggest that '2D is dead'. Driessen resists this idea by engaging with the mutual presentation of 2D flat planes and the illusion of 3D volumes in the same drawn space.

Richard Reeves is an experimental film-maker at Quickdraw Animation Society (QAS) in Calgary, Canada. He works in the tradition of Norman McLaren, mark-making directly on to film stock. This mark-making works as a particular model of drawing, and is configured to explore pattern-making and formalist experimentation with line, colour and form. Reeves remarks: 'During 1978–79 I attended Sault College of Applied Arts & Technology. I was inspired by the artwork of the Group of Seven, and the school is located in a region where many of their sketches were made. However, for some reason I became bored of school and decided to travel. Drawing became a type of diary for the journeys, and I was able to create paintings for solo or group shows during winter hibernation…. Between travelling and working I found time to explore slide photography combined with music, which eventually led to film animation.'

Reeves soon realised that he was not attracted to becoming a traditional animator, and that his work and attitude would find greater purchase within a tradition of experimental film-making: 'I recognised animation as an art form, to be the perfect mix of drawing and music. In 1989 I discovered the QAS in Calgary. It was here that I was exposed to a large variety of animation techniques and resources…. Although I had watched some Saturday morning cartoons growing up, it was not until seeing work by Norman McLaren and other NFB art films that I realised how animation can be personal and the images as unique as the artist's style. The concept of motion painting, visual music and making drawings come alive became a happy obsession.'

▼

Reeves at work

Reeves working directly with, and on, film stock, extending the parameters of drawing for animation.

Reeves strongly felt that there needed to be an alternative tradition to standard cartoons: 'While corporations are creating large studio productions designed for making television series and feature films, these highly advertised and marketed animations seem to dominate public culture. They usually have anthropomorphic characters that act and respond like humans. There seems also to be trends in creating animated characters that begin to take on a highly realistic appearance, using sophisticated digital technology and very large budgets. To me it is interesting that animation can be taken in such a direction.'

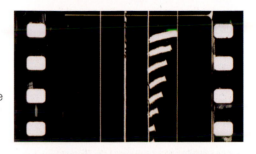

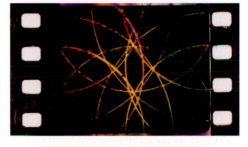

▶

Abstract compositions

animator
Richard Reeves

A range of Richard Reeves's abstract compositions on individual film frames in which he explores the interfaces between lines, colours and patterns.

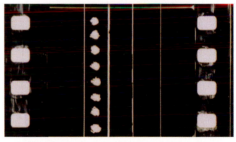

Paul Driessen > **Richard Reeves** > Michael Dudok de Wit

He continues, 'However, animation is a small word with a large interpretation, where both concept and technique can bring about unique experiences…. Animated films can illuminate the subconscious and transcend daily thoughts. This is the type of animation that excites me the most, and unfortunately this type of animation is not as accessible as the mainstream cartoons. For some years now, my personal animations have been created by drawing directly on to motion-picture film…there seems to be an inexhaustible amount of technical applications to create images and sounds on the film's surface. The whole notion of making a camera-less film is completed by having an accompanied drawn-on film soundtrack.

Reeves is particularly preoccupied with soundtrack because it shares the same conditions as working with the visual images on the surface of the frame: 'Usually I create the hand-drawn soundtrack first, then draw the images to the sounds. This helps to match the visual tempo with the musical rhythms. The sounds are usually produced by some sort of intuitive process that is suited to the concept or theme, and relies upon trusting my basic instinct and what I find interesting.'

▼

Colour experiments

animator
Richard Reeves

Reeves's forte is in colour experimentation, combining different colour tonalities in vivid contrast.

  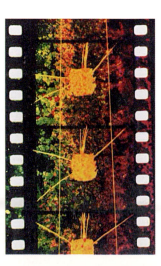

Reeves's *Sea Song* (1999) is highly regarded for its political commitment, still something that is not readily associated with abstract film, despite it often being a motivating aspect of wanting to work experimentally in the first instance. He remarks: '1998 was the international year of the ocean, and this became the inspiration for *Sea Song*. I also wanted to express some environmental concerns (pollution, over-fishing, nuclear submarines, etc). During this time I had moved to a small island off the coast of British Columbia, near Vancouver. Taking walks along the seaside – especially at night, sketching by flashlight or during full moons – I was able to collect enough drawings to create a rough storyboard of the ideas gathered. I like to leave room during the creation process to allow for improvising or stream of consciousness, and I am usually working on different sections at different times in a non-linear fashion.'

Reeves stresses: 'The camera-less animations of Norman McLaren and Evelyn Lambart have been very influential, especially ones with animated hand-drawn sounds. McLaren seems to have invented a language by drawing sound that we can expand upon. My personal favorites are the trance-like *Mosaic* (1965) by Norman McLaren and Evelyn Lambart and the energised *Particles in Space* (1979) by Len Lye. These animations demonstrate the power of abstract imagery drawn on to film by their effect on the imagination.

'Other significant influences have been the animations of Oskar Fischinger and Mary Ellen Bute. These animators demonstrated to me how one can have the creative independence of a painter and express with line, form and colour to illustrate motion paintings.'

Biography of Richard Reeves

age 4   age 8   age 10

age 12   age 18   age 21

age 24   age 27   age 30

age 33   age 36   today

◄

Autobiographical storyboard

animator
Richard Reeves

Reeves creates a storyboard of his own experience, from his drawing at school to growing up to be an animator, and then ultimately drawing directly on film to achieve camera-less animation.

Michael Dudok de Wit's approach is all about using what might be termed the 'lyrical line' to evoke complex memories and contemplative pleasures. Dudok de Wit notes: 'I've had a passion for drawing since early childhood and one of the graphic styles that inspired me most was the clean line, as in the comic strips by Hergé and Edgar P Jacobs. My artistic mother was a great inspiration too. At art college I specialised in etching first and in animation and photography later.'

This 'clean line' is a far cry from the dirty aesthetic pursued by Cook (see page 170), but in the same way it is seeking the same kind of distillation in its suggestion and meaning. This kind of purity has little in common with classical Disney drawing, however: 'The classic Disney styles are more elaborate and they involve more drawing skill and more complex animation than mine. Disney characters talk a lot and they have well defined facial features with large, expressive eyes. So far, I have created simple characters with dot-shaped eyes and sometimes even without a mouth.'

Dudok de Wit, then, seeks to pare down the scale of mark-making to make the most from a minimalist palette, using the line for more associative and symbolic means.

title
Father and Daughter

animator
Michael Dudok de Wit

Michael Dudok de Wit's *Father and Daughter* (2000) uses simple line forms to suggest the most powerful and affecting of elementals and their place in memories.

Drawing characters and concepts

Of his masterpiece, *Father and Daughter*, he recalls: 'I started by writing the story down. Next came three visual stages in the development of the film: the sketch stage, the design stage and the storyboard stage. Once I had gone through these I had a solid story and I could begin with the animation and the backgrounds. During the sketch stage I made rough sketches to get a feel of the project. I drew landscapes from memory or from photographs. They were not necessarily nice drawings and I had no obligation to show them to anyone. The second stage – designing the characters and some of the landscapes – involved a lot of research. I assembled an abundance of reference images and videos, for instance of cyclists and birds, clouds, flat landscapes, trees, period clothing, in order to distil this information into a simple selection. I also searched for a technique that I had not used before. Charcoal was new to me, but I quickly found it an extremely pleasant tool. It was fast and intuitive to use, it gave a great texture, and with the help of Photoshop I could give the artwork the desired contrast and colours.

'The storyboard was drawn with soft pencil on animation paper. I drew each picture separately, cut it out, positioned it on the table with a handful of other storyboard drawings and worked out the right sequence. For each final storyboard page I drew the pictures again, this time in the right order on an A3-sized sheet, four drawings per sheet. The storyboard stage lasted several months, which is relatively long. This was due to the large number of drawings and also to the time it took me to think about the narrative flow. The challenge was to condense a long life from early childhood till old age into an eight-minute film while avoiding a hectic pace, and to achieve this I kept the story as simple as possible. Integrating images of nature helped a lot too, I think. Not just because they softened the big jumps in the story, but also because nature has that ability to remind us of timelessness and eternity.'

title
Father and Daughter

animator
Michael Dudok de Wit

Dudok de Wit shows that, while individual loss is inevitable, life itself goes on. Even the most powerful of bonds is but small in the face of the bigger elemental and spiritual experience informing the human condition.

Richard Reeves > **Michael Dudok de Wit** > Luis Cook

Dudok de Wit's sensitive use of the Dutch landscape hints at other painterly traditions but, crucially, speaks to the tone, texture and dynamic of drawing as a prompt in the recollection of primal feeling and memory. This has the consequence of making the story visualisation highly emotive: 'I didn't have a precise method, but the following classic technique was useful: I would pin some of the storyboard drawings, and eventually all of them, on the wall, and I would follow the sequence of drawings with my eyes at the same pace as I wanted the story to unfold itself in the film. I would visualise the film at the right speed, imagining the animated movements and some of the crucial sound effects. That gave me a better idea of the choreography, the emotions and the suspense. I would do this over and over again while I was storyboarding, but also during the animation phase.'

This technique insists upon letting time inform the nature of the perception and understanding of the imagery, which demands a highly empathic response.

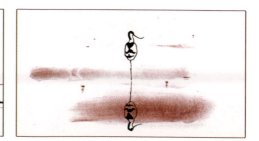

title
Father and Daughter

animator
Michael Dudok de Wit

Dudok de Wit evokes the deep love shared by a father and daughter through the sepia-tinged passing of time.

De Wit recalls, too: 'In *Father and Daughter* I could not use any verbal language to help the narrative or to accentuate the emotions, because I had chosen to make a dialogue-free film. But film language is so rich; like many film-makers I tried to use the combined effect of different aspects of film-making – like the lighting; the colour scheme; the ambience of the landscapes and the relationship between the character and the landscape in each scene; the point of view of the camera; the presence of nature; the overall timing; and especially the acting; the use of music and of sound – to express emotions. It was my aim to use the feeling of longing as the main emotion; in fact, that drove me to make the film in the first place. I find deep longing quietly painful, but also incredibly beautiful, and I thought: wouldn't it be amazing to make a film about pure longing?'

Dudok de Wit's achievement lies in the way his engagement with the primal nature of mark-making captures and comprehends the pleasure and pain in yearning and need. The immediacy of the lyrical line belies the deep-seated memories it evokes; it is at the very heart of the feelings of love and loss that characterise our closest bonds and relationships.

Richard Reeves > **Michael Dudok de Wit** > Luis Cook

Luis Cook is one of Aardman Animation's most talented animators. His multi-award-winning film, *The Pearce Sisters* (2007), reflects a maturing of his graphic sensibility and narrative ingenuity. Of his childhood, Cook recalls: 'I did a lot of drawing with my dad as a child. He would bring home computer paper from work. It was thin with perforated edges. He bought me books on Hieronymus Bosch and Jackson Pollock. Bosch's *The Garden of Earthly Delights* scared the hell out of me. At that time I preferred Albrecht Dürer and would meticulously reproduce his woodcuts. I much preferred his drawing to his painting. It seemed lighter, relaxed and more accessible. My love of drawing came from my inability to be good at anything else. I was average at most things. Drawing was the one area I excelled in.'

Having discovered this talent, Cook went to art college: 'I was taught drawing by a Japanese minimalist. He would make us draw with our left hand standing on one foot for hours on end. He would make it as physically demanding as possible. He never said a word. We had to reach our own conclusions. The principle was to unlearn, explore mark-making and embrace the unexpected. The end results were awkward, accidental, spirited and unusual. I had started to really appreciate "bad" drawing.'

title
The Pearce Sisters

animator
Luis Cook

Cook's film *The Pearce Sisters* achieves an original styling by echoing the 'bad' drawing of early cultures and outsider art.

I often decide on a few key words that I will stick to. Ugly. Beautiful. Slow. Negation. Atmosphere. Colour. Drawing and drawing. There are no short cuts, really. You just have to sit and draw.

Luis Cook

Drawing characters and concepts

Cook's unique approach – essentially a resistance to established idioms of classical animation informed by his experience and observation – confirms the versatility of the form, and suggests that drawing can be discovered, used and configured in different, but no less interesting or useful ways. Cook has the insular talents of the outsider artist, absolutely focused on the specificity of aesthetic he wishes to achieve. Cook's work is a far cry from Disney's classical styling: 'I was never trained classically. I studied animation at the Royal College of Art, but that is not the same thing. At the RCA they nurture the individual voice, not a studio voice. As a result I come to drawn animation from a position of ignorance. I know very little about Disney or studio techniques, although I do now appreciate Disney through my daughter's eyes. I am more a designer/director and try to ignore animation constraints, at least at the early drawing stage. Starting from the script and working backwards from the most relevant/ interesting image I can come up with. Only at this point do I then try to figure out how it might be achieved through animation. Then, it could be anything – 2D, 3D stop-motion; live action; mixed media – hopefully something I hadn't tried before.'

Michael Dudok de Wit > **Luis Cook** > Gerrit van Dijk

the pearce sisters

Like a number of the animators presented in this chapter, Cook trusts his intuition, and his instinctive responses to a script or concept. He shares with Richard Reeves an attraction to stream of consciousness in his work, although he does give himself some aesthetic guides: 'I often decide on a few key words that I will stick to. Ugly. Beautiful. Slow. Negation. Atmosphere. Colour. Drawing and drawing. There are no short cuts, really. You just have to sit and draw. Sometimes it comes naturally, other times it feels like hard graft. It is abstract problem-solving. Trying to solve a puzzle that has no conclusive answer. Just a feeling that something is right. Sometimes music helps to jolt you in another direction or to set a tone in your head. Different mediums help: charcoal, ink, paint, collage; or drawing with your left hand. Drawing in front of the TV as quickly as you can, not looking at the paper, just the images as they fly by. At some point something interesting emerges and you work it up until it becomes natural.'

Development of such highly personal processes inevitably enables auteurs to emerge within animation – something that drawing inherently encourages. Cook notes: 'From a film-making point of view, drawn animation is attractive because it can be more authored, more personal, more idiosyncratic. It is painstaking, yes, but it is also freer, more organic and immediate. This is a blessing and a curse. If done well it can draw the audience into new worlds and unusual aesthetics. It can also keep an audience out far more than other forms of animation. It can be more demanding to watch. I'm not sure why, maybe because it is illustrative. The audience must be more aware that this is an illustration of a story, many steps removed from reality. They must have to work harder to engage with the narrative. It's caught between fine art and film narrative. A difficult place to tread. An old tutor of mine once said, "Film is prose. Animation is poetry." For me, drawn animation is the most poetic of all. It's somehow richer, denser, and has a strong link to childhood memory, to picture books, to painting, to impossible worlds.'

◀

**Storyboard for
The Pearce Sisters**

animator
Luis Cook

Part of Cook's storyboard for *The Pearce Sisters*, using iconic elements to promote a particular suggestion of unease, disturbance and alienation.

Michael Dudok de Wit > **Luis Cook** > Gerrit van Dijk

The Pearce Sisters plays with a number of aesthetic and technical contradictions: 'I wanted to tell a simple story. I wanted to experiment with computer-generated (CG) and drawn animation, to rough it up, to personalise the CG animation somehow. I wanted to bring together high- and low-tech animation techniques. I wanted the film to have a strong bleak atmosphere. I wanted it to be funny and sad. I wanted it to look ugly and beautiful. To be modern and old-fashioned, repellent and engaging, naive and sophisticated. I wanted to make a film that felt as if it had been washed up by the sea.'

To achieve these prosaic and poetic ends, Cook looked to his work in drawing: 'Drawing was used from the beginning to the end of production. I drew initial designs. I drew storyboards. I drew an animatic, working out the shots, the shot lengths and the compositions, all black and white and very rough. I then produced a full-colour design for all 188 shots in the film. This was an experimental process; we hadn't done it before and I wanted to reduce the room for error. In CG we lined up the animation to these designs, using the design as a 2D background. We even pulled the characters around, making them deliberately inconsistent in each shot. Once a shot was animated in the computer the frames were then printed out and we drew over the top. The results were then scanned back in and composited over the CG. We also projected drawn elements on to the CG models, or drew directly on to them.

'The final result is primarily a 2D film, but one that is informed by all the volume and dimension 3D can achieve. It is a curious mix which I hope contributes to the unsettling atmosphere of the film. In short, everything was drawn. Even the titles and credits were hand-drawn.'

title
The Pearce Sisters

artist
Luis Cook

Here the Pearce sisters seek to
revive the body of a man they
recover from the sea. The off-
centre nature of the characters
and the narrative places
events in the far distance or,
alternatively, sometimes in
extreme close-up. The gothic
imperatives of the narrative
are always underpinning the
mise-en-scène by suggestion.

Michael Dudok de Wit > Luis Cook > Gerrit van Dijk

Gerrit van Dijk is one of Holland's foremost animators, and one of animation's true iconoclasts and characters. In a spirit of advising students about drawing, he drew the top 10 tips shown on page 176.

Van Dijk is clear that the dominant American cartoon tradition does not provide the only form of expression available to animators. In revering the work of McLaren, and the ways in which drawing itself becomes the most direct vehicle for the expression of thoughts and feelings, van Dijk made *I Move, So I Am* (1998), an autobiographical testimony to his own engagement and investment in drawing, and the profound influences of the culture around him. Further, the film becomes a recognition of the ways in which animation works as a vehicle for evidencing memory and illustrating experience.

▼ ▶

Letter to Norman McLaren

author
Gerrit van Dijk

Gerrit van Dijk's letter to Norman McLaren acknowledges his influence, and cites his desire to make a film called *I Move, So I Am*.

Haarlem 5 december 1997

brief aan:
Norman Mc Laren.

Beste Norman

„Ego cogito, Ergo Sum„, denkt René Decartes als deze, in geduld poseert voor Frans Hals, de kunstschilder alhier.
Decartes ziet het gezicht van de schilder, tussen diens waarneming en hoe dit je verbeelden.
Zijn, ego cogito, ergo sum, wordt: Ego Sum, ergo exito, of te wel: je pense, donc je Suis„
Het resultaat van deze posarsessie in het atelier van Hals is een prachtig openwiseld portret van een denkend mens en valt te bewonderen in het Louvre te Parijs.
Doch jij, Norman, gaat verder dan René Decartes, als je zegt: When you animate a creature, is the creature a movie, you are that: you feel that motion„
Beter is het niet te duiden.
Daarom krijgt de film, die ik nu bezig ben te maken, de titel:„ I move, so I am„, en waarin ik Decartes gedachten, aangaande de mens zijn waarnemingen en lerkaan combineer met die van jou.
Een ieder tracht zijn waarnemingen vorm te geven, de schrijver-filosoof in woorden, de kunstenaar in beelden en de animatiefilmer in bewegende beelden. Deze beelden geven dan wederom nieuwe waarnemingen aan de toeschouwer.
Zo ga ik in „ I move, so I am„, een klein gedeelte uit jou film „Hen Hop„ gebruiken als metafoor voor mijn eigen waarnemingen bij het aanschouwen van werk van anderen. Werk wat mijner bewustzijn verruimde en inspireerde tot nieuwe beelden.
Het gezicht, welk plaats vindt tussen waarnemen en hoe het te verbeelden, van de mens in het algemeen

202

en de creatieve in het bizonder, is de inspiratie en het ne heilige moeten, om de film „I move, so I am„ te maken, of beter gezegd: te scheppen.
Dit gedeelte uit „Hen Hop„ ga ik ongevraagd gebruiken.
Immers zou ik om toestemming vragen zou dit duiden op een twijfel mijnerzijds.

Norman, dat de wil en inspiratie tot het scheppen van nieuwe beelden & bewegingen, nog heel lang Uw deel moge zijn
zij U gewenst
in grote vriendschap

Je toegenegen
GERRIT

Haarlem, 5 December 1997

Dear Norman

René Descartes thinks "Ego cogito, ergo sum" while he is patiently posing for Frans Hals, the local painter.

Descartes sees the struggle of the painter between his observation and how to represent it.

His "ego cogito, ergo sum" becomes "ego sum, ergo exito" or "je pense, donc je suis".

The result of this posing session in the atelier of Hals is a beautifully painted portrait of a thinking man that can be admired in the Louvre in Paris.

But you, Norman, take it a step further than René Descartes when you say: "When you animate a creature, the creature is a pure motion, and you are that; you feel that motion." One cannot interpret it any better.

That's why the title of film I'm making at the moment, will be "I Move, So I Am", in which I combine Descartes' thoughts about man, his consciousness and existence with yours.

Everybody tries to give shape to his observations: the writer-philosopher with words, the artist with images, and the animation film-maker in moving images.

These images then again give the spectator new perceptions.

So I will use in "I Move, So I Am" a little fragment from your film "Hen Hop" (1942) as a metaphor for my own perceptions when I watch the work of others, work that awoke my consciousness and inspired to new images.

The battle taking place between the perceived observation and how to represent it, of men in general, and the creative artist in particular, is the inspiration to make the film "I Move, So I Am". Or a better way to say it: to create.

I will use this part from "Hen Hop" without asking. Asking for permission means that I have to hesitate.

Norman, may the will and inspiration to create new images and motions fall to you to share for a long time.

Wished to you in great friendship.

Yours affectionately,

Gerrit

Luis Cook > Gerrit van Dijk

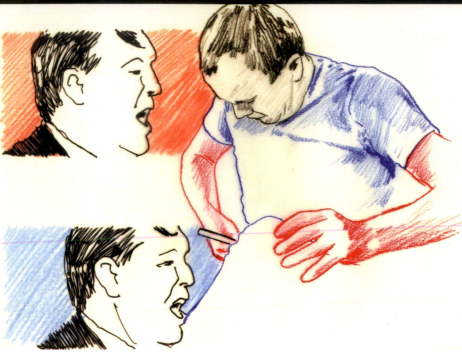

▲

title
I Move, So I Am

animator
Gerrit van Dijk

Van Dijk animates himself in the
literal act of drawing himself,
while recalling the iconic figure of
Bill Haley, his youth, and the
rhythmic influence of rock
and roll.

Drawing characters and concepts

title
I Move, So I Am

animator
Gerrit van Dijk

Van Dijk recognises the impact of religious experience and the struggle for faith, here symbolised through his ongoing 'self-construction', and the iconic presence of the cross and the figure of Jesus.

title
I Move, So I Am

animator
Gerrit van Dijk

Van Dijk signals the indigenous and aesthetic influence of Piet Mondrian in relation to modernist forms and idioms, and its impact on more abstract forms of animation.

title
I Move, So I Am

animator
Gerrit van Dijk

Van Dijk's most explicit reference to Norman McLaren's film, *Hen Hop*, in which McLaren's empathy with the hen translates directly into his drawing for animation. This is, of course, echoed in van Dijk's drawing of himself throughout the film.

Luis Cook > Gerrit van Dijk

Abstraction
Non-linear, non-objective, purely abstract drawing investigating forms, shapes and colours for their own sake is of considerable importance in animation.

Action and reaction
Most action in animation is in some way caricatured or exaggerated as a clear 'event' which prompts a reaction. Primary action normally consists of forward movement played out through the whole of the body, while secondary action is generally the effects on specific parts of the body or on other figures and objects in the environment, which can often necessitate an equal and opposite reaction.

Anatomical studies
Animators use anatomical studies of people and animals to help them construct realistic motion for a character, based on the extension of limbs, weight proportions, landing strides, etc.

Animal representation
Animal characters combine human and animal traits, which enables deeper characterisation. By not casting and creating human figures, animated films can also circumvent many social, religious and cultural taboos.

Animatics
A filmed synthesis of storyboard panels with a provisional soundtrack to create a mock version of the animation to gauge if the narrative works, what might need to be added or removed, and how the dialogue, music, etc might potentially work in relation to the suggested images.

Annecy Film Festival
The first and biggest animation festival in the world bringing together the arts and commercial sectors in a celebration of animation of all styles, techniques and approaches, and informed by historical and contemporary work (www.annecy.org).

Anthropomorphise
The endowment of human characteristics on animals, objects and environments.

Anticipation
A model of signifying the movement that is to follow. Before moving in one direction, a figure or object moves back in the opposite direction, effectively pre-figuring the move and offering it greater clarity and emphasis.

Auteur
Auteur theory was espoused during the 1950s and promoted the view of the film director as the sole author of a film, and as a figure with consistent thematic and aesthetic concerns across a body of work. It can be pertinently applied to animation film-makers who often create the whole work themselves.

Cartoon
A contentious term in animation, as it has become singularly associated with the American animated cartoon, thus limiting understanding of the form. The term 'animation' is often preferred because it is more readily associated with a variety of other styles and techniques, as well as production in other nations. Fundamental to the cartoon form is the 'drawing' which underpins it.

Character
The way in which a person acts and behaves, and is spiritually, morally, socially and practically developed through the choices he or she makes.

Compositing
Simply, compositing is the combining of images from a variety of possible sources within the same frame, to either achieve a seamless blend or a deliberate counterpoint. This is in essence a layering system, although it's always part of the special effects processes in film from its early configurations, it has become an integral part of the production and editorial process in the digital era.

Dope sheet
A planning tool for animators that allows all intended visualised action and sound to be broken down by frame, scene and sequence to provide instructions to the rest of the team. Also known as an exposure sheet or a camera-instruction sheet.

Endotropic shadow
Shading that occurs inside and on the form.

Exotropic shadow
Shading that occurs outside and defines the form.

Floating World painters
Ukiyo-e art (literally translates as 'pictures of the floating world'), originated in shogun-era Tokyo, and celebrated urban cultural pleasures. Hokusai, the most well known of the Floating World artists, inflected his work with more of a pastoral idyll.

Gaze

A resonant term in both film study and art history that may refer to the artist's interpretive and creative act of seeing, or the audience's way of seeing – scopophilic, invasive, controlling, voyeuristic, etc. Ownership of the gaze and the mode of looking may underpin the creation of politically and ideologically charged representational forms.

Hyperrealism

Disney's classical animation style combines caricatural excess to signify personality and a level of realism in anatomy and motion to add conviction to the figure's behaviour and identity.
It underpins the animation style of contemporary computer-animated imagery.

Illustration

The narrative drawing that supports the specific interpretation of a text or concept, predicated on static, graphic principles that literally interpret or associatively suggest story events and development.

Key frame poses

The start and end points, plus other significant points of structural change, of a choreographed motion, which must then be 'in-betweened' to create a fully animated sequence.

Layout

Provides a background to the action, and may also offer a mapping or performative element if shot in a specific way. Layout is a pertinent aspect of visualisation when allied to choreographed moves.

Mise-en-scène

The nature and construction of the material content of the image. In animation, the normal conventions of the physical and performance space are in flux so that animated events – a gag, a specific image, an abstract form, etc – stand out.

Model (or character) sheet

A sheet outlining the size and construction of an animated character's design from a number of viewing perspectives, and including detail about face, hands, feet, etc. This enables a number of animators working across a production to achieve consistency in representation.

Negative space

The area of an image that is not occupied by a definitive shape or form, but which gives meaning to the foregrounded figure. This might be the background, but is more often shadow.

Process

Drawing can reveal the thought processes behind the act of creativity, as well as the experience of the artist as the drawing unfolds, as seen in the work of Michael Shaw and William Kentridge.

Satiric caricature

Political cartooning that offers insight about, and mockery of, political and cultural figures and institutions.

Sign

A visual signifier of specific social and cultural information and/or meaning; much is made of the role of signs in semiotic analysis.

'Squash 'n' stretch'

Typical to Disney animation, characters' bodies are configured as a series of circles that compress and extend as they move. This enables exaggerated movement that remains relatively natural, and demonstrates how gravity, weight, speed, space and distance work to determine movement.

Stereotype

Characterisation that is informed by only one dominant characteristic, or plays out social stereotypes. Animation can both interrogate these typologies and, more often, create more complex characters defined by their interior states.

Visualisation

Visualisation stresses only the pictorial, and works differently from, or complementarily with, dialogue and written descriptors. Visualisation processes are determined by the technique chosen, the concept engaged with and the intention of the narrative.

Weight and speed

Weight dictates speed: larger characters tend to move more slowly, and their posture is more affected by their weight, while shorter and/or thinner characters tend to move more quickly.

The focus of the book has been to suggest that there are many more uses for, and applications of, drawing in animation than simply the long-established classical approach. While Disney-style full animation has informed the art of character animation since the 1920s and remains an intrinsic aspect of the form, a comprehensive account of classical animation has not been provided here – that is best written of elsewhere (see Bibliography). It is, however, a touchstone to the place of other drawing styles and drawing as a creative tool. This book has sought to offer advice to reduce the intimidation that the demands of classical drawing in animation places upon potential animators and to demonstrate how, by thinking differently and using drawing in other ways, it is possible to animate through other approaches.

The act of learning to draw has been encouraged throughout this book and there is little doubt that, with practice, dedication and focused aesthetic intention, the quality of what is drawn improves. Constantly observing everyday life, embracing material from all aspects of the media, persistently seeking to ask questions and solve problems, learning from mistakes, and previsualising the intended work are all crucial to being successful in drawing for animation. It is also the case that learning from 'the greats', many of whom appear or are referenced in this book, is absolutely vital.

Tim Fernée, Bill Plympton and Deanna Marsigliese are all fine actors working through the medium of the pencil; their animated stage is perpetually freshened and reinvented by the primal nature of expressing through mark-making the most contemporary of concerns, contexts and cultures. Here they share their notes on drawing.

Tim Fernée

Tim Fernée has considerable experience in the animation industry, and his expertise is well acknowledged, so it is a surprise when his advice is prefaced with an interesting admission: 'My own drawing ability is limited. I can draw quickly – which is a strength in animation – but my weakness is, when I slow down, the drawings get worse! Consequently, I should feel fraudulent pontificating about how to draw well for animation. But I have had to give some thought as to how drawn animation works, simply to make the best of what drawing ability I have.'

This is a very important observation in the sense that it is important to match innate skill with the demands of the task, informed by the best advice. As an experienced animator, therefore, Fernée offers the following tips:

▶ Know how things work
However well you can draw, you cannot possibly animate a movement – mechanical or organic – that you do not understand. Mastering movement in this way will help your animation make the most of your drawing.

▶ Understand the process
Drawing for animation is akin to drawing for printing. Some aspects of your drawings are emphasised; others are lost. Even an untreated sketch or hand-rendered animation takes on a life of its own when it is shot and, nowadays, you are far more likely to be drawing into software. Whatever the process, understand it and turn it to your advantage.

▶

title
The Marsh King's Daughter

animator
Tim Fernée

Ink and digipainting pushed further to evoke the world of fairy tale and classic children's illustration.

▶ Understand timing

This is not only the essence of drama but also of believability – conveying such physicalities as weight, scale and distance. Good drawing will not yield convincing animation without good timing (some of the earliest animation is beautifully drawn but doesn't work because timing had yet to be understood), whereas good timing can bring to life imperfect drawings.

▶ Memory – analysis

Try to understand the relationship between animation and memory. Animation requires drawings based on observation, but the chord they must strike is in the memory or imagination of the audience. Even a walk or run will be unconvincing to someone who remembers the action differently, and once you have to explain to an audience (or client) that something they think looks wrong is actually right, you are lost, Muybridge notwithstanding....

▶ Teamwork

Drawing for animation is almost always a team enterprise. It is legitimate to select colleagues who help conceal your (and one another's) inadequacies; indeed, it is a necessary skill, without which you cannot make a film longer or better than you yourself can draw!

▶ Drawing as a development tool

As animation production becomes less dependent upon drawing, those of us who draw obsessively find ourselves increasingly involved in the visual thinking-through that is development, presenting us with wonderful opportunities to create visual narrative and challenging us to make our visual thinking ever clearer and more accessible.

D'Eon 'twixt the shafts - he's shafted again

◀

title
Rowlandson Rides Again

animator
Tim Fernée

Frame from *Rowlandson Rides Again* whose sketch-like combination of pencil and Photoshop evokes the artist's rumbustious Regency world so effectively it ended up in the politically incorrect section of the Annecy Film Festival.

Bill Plympton

Bill Plympton is one of the leading comedy animation auteurs and is revered for his particular style of cartooning. Here he identifies a dozen key ideas which he believes are important in relation to drawing for animation:

▶ Draw all the time.

▶ Learn how to draw faces, feet, hands and fabric.

▶ Draw from TV.

▶ Use shadows.

▶ Have a kid's curiosity.

▶ Find a unique style.

▶ Be observant of life.

▶ Carry a pencil and pad everywhere.

▶ Love the mistakes.

▶ Draw scenes from all different angles.

▶ Steal from the greats.

▶ Visualise the image in your mind before drawing.

Plympton established his reputation and style through drawing political cartoons and working in illustration, although he did not become an animator until later in his career. He recalls: 'As an illustrator and cartoonist, I had built up over the years a pile of funny ideas for animated films; it was just a question of drawing them. All those years pent up, not being an animator, made me feel I was way behind schedule; that I had missed the boat and needed to catch up. I went back through my old ideas and made short films, one every two or three months or so. (*One Of Those Days* (1988), for example, came out of a cartoon that I did for a men's magazine. It was the last things that famous people saw before they died – it was really popular.) People have said that I am very prolific but it was those 15 years not doing animation that made me want to get my ideas out there and find an audience.'

▶

title
Idiots and Angels

artist
Bill Plympton

A sample of images from *Idiots and Angels*. Plympton's signature style figures feature in typically sparse environments, but unusually here, in a more sombrely toned and coloured mise-en-scène.

Plympton remembers fondly his first forays in the understanding of the animated form, and underlines here the significance of using published sources to enhance technique and approach: 'I was obsessed with The Mickey Mouse Club. I joined the club and got the magazine – I thought that was the height of animation. I thought some characters were really appealing through being well drawn – especially in something like *The Jungle Book*. My aunt took me to Disneyland when I was 12 or 13. The thing I remember most was wanting this Walt Disney animation book in the shop. It just goes to show how single-minded I was about being an animator. I wanted to see this book and find out how these guys made these films. It was a rational response to me.'

He also stresses the importance of embracing opportunities to practise and learn in the development of a craft: 'When I moved to New York in 1975, I managed to draw political cartoons for the *SoHo Weekly News*. This was the Ford era, which compelled everyone to be politicised, so my art became politicised. I soon became bored with it though, and I was not very good at it; I was unusual too, because I did a continuity strip, not a single-box cartoon. But I was doing a lot of other things – the sex cartoons for the men's magazines; commercial illustrations, lots.'

Plympton's independence and free-spiritedness has informed his career and output, enabled him to resist being absorbed into one of the major studios and to continue working with his own signature drawing style.

A webcam on Plympton's website allows over-the-shoulder access to his drawing and approach on his latest feature, *Idiots and Angels*, and provides a useful learning tool.

Deanna Marsigliese

If Fernée and Plympton offer advice as experienced practitioners, it is useful to conclude this section with some points from Deanna Marsigliese, who not only creates her own work, but is a dedicated teacher of animation.

Although classically trained, she explains: 'I have developed my artistic skills by drawing constantly and working closely with talented peers, instructors and colleagues. I don't believe that drawing for animation is concerned with any one style in particular. Animation drawings are defined by their purpose; to convey life, story, movement. Each drawing should feel like it is part of an ongoing sequence, displaying a sense of force, direction, weight, clarity and, of course, emotion. Regardless of one's drawing style, drawing for animation involves dynamics; conveying a sense of energy and life.'

Marsigliese offers the following advice regarding dynamics in animation:

▶ Your lines should come together to convey movement and emotion, giving a sense of life to each storytelling pose. It is important to stay loose.

▶ Always draw from the shoulder, rather than your wrist. This will give you more freedom and movement, allowing you to sketch broader, more dynamic gestural lines.

▶ When posing for animation, it is a good idea to lay down a structural foundation using a line of action. This allows for a greater sense of direction, force and balance right from the very beginning. Use this line to give your drawings fluidity and unity.

▶ As you continue to flush out the pose, be aware of your volumes, proportions and overall silhouette.

▶ Be economical with your lines to avoid noodling, using darker strokes to convey tension and weight.

▶ Stay gestural.

▶ Poses should appear effortless and dynamic.

▶ Do not labour over your work.

▶ Unnecessary lines and details will stiffen the drawing and interrupt the rhythm.

Marsigliese argues that animation drawing should be not merely functional, but also informed by the technical dexterity of its execution and a versatile language of expression: 'My drawing processes vary depending on the project. When I draw specifically for an animated sequence I use a combination of all of the above points. I am a great believer in research. I often tell my students to dedicate at least one-third of their allotted time to the analysis of the movement and/or the emotions portrayed. This will allow you to draw with accuracy. It is important to take inspiration from life and to carry it into your character poses. Afterward, I will use my intuition to enhance my drawings through caricature, pushing and pulling the shapes and lines, adding weight and exaggeration as needed. Finally, I will explore the poses further, adding creative touches and details. It's very helpful to lay the "technical", more accurate foundations down first, then layer them with caricature and exaggeration.

'When character-designing for animation, I find that my approach is purely intuitive. I may begin with little direction and experiment with the use of different shapes, colours and lines, choosing combinations that will best depict that character's personality. It is important to read the script, note the dialogue, and get a sense of your character's mannerisms, habits and overall demeanour. In my opinion, your character is only as believable as you imagine him or her to be. When designing, do so with appeal: clean shapes, fun proportions, contrasting straights and curves, lines that show form and movement. Different approaches to these principles can be seen in the works of other artists you admire. When in need of more inspiration, I will take it from life. Being surrounded by other people allows me to capture their characteristics, facial features and body types in my design work. Drawing on textured surfaces with new colours and media also encourages accidental effects and unique ways of approaching a design. Finally, it is important to create within a state of timelessness; to relax, explore and have fun.'

Playful design

artist
Deanna Marsigliese

Marsigliese's sense of fun emerges in these playful images of mermaids and caricatures of The Beatles.

At the outset of this project, I discussed with Joanna Quinn and Les Mills how we might collaborate on a book. Joanna wished to bring her own sense of the pure joy and intrinsic skills of drawing to the project, while Les wished to add his thoughts on relating narrative and concept to the drawing enterprise. I wanted to add 'the bigger picture', determined to move the subject of 'drawing for animation' beyond the technical manuals largely concerned with reiterating classical animation techniques, and the seemingly singular association of 'drawing' with 'the cartoon'. What was important for all three authors was to offer some practical tools, some critical analysis, and encouragement to experiment with and embrace all kinds of different models of drawing for animation. We hope we have achieved this aim.

Quinn herself has become an acknowledged master of animation, and the colleagues within the field represented here, among them de Wit, Driessen, Plympton and Cook, for example, all share a mutual respect and admiration for each other's achievements. More significantly, though, all wish to engage with the breadth of visual influences from comic strips to fine art; illustration to primitive forms; political cartooning to animation itself, and embrace all related art forms from dance to sculpture to theatre. This willingness to use all manner of visual cultures in the service of animation is crucial in the development of core skills and knowledge and the creation of a distinctive work; work that in this instance springs from the versatility of the drawn form and the unique expression available through animation.

This book has sought to offer a range of trajectories so that drawing for animation will be understood as a complex and varied form operating in numerous contexts, and not merely that of classical animation in the Disney style. A key intention – essentially the desire to help cultivate the ability to translate a significantly expressive feeling or thought on to paper and into motion – is effectively at the heart of this discussion. Drawing can evidence memories, thoughts, emotions and speculation, and it is truly the 'bodily stuff' in communicating our complex and demanding inner characters, landscapes and signs. Drawing remains the fundamental language of expression underpinning all forms of animation even in the digital era; mark-making will continue to be the most primal and formative of expressions, and animation its most sophisticated vehicle in the creation of meaning and effect.

▼

United Airlines advertisement

artist
Joanna Quinn

Key texts

Hart, C (1997)
How to Draw Animation
New York: Watson-Guptill Publications

Missal, S (2004)
Exploring Drawing For Animation
New York: Thomson Delmar Learning

Whitaker H & Halas, J (2002)
Timing for Animation
Boston & Oxford: Focal Press

White, T (1999)
The Animator's Workbook
New York: Watson-Guptill Publications

Williams, R (2001)
The Animator's Survival Kit
London & Boston: Faber & Faber

Animation history

Adams, TR (1991)
Tom and Jerry: 50 Years of Cat and Mouse
New York: Crescent Books

Adamson, J (1974)
Tex Avery: King of Cartoons
New York: Da Capo

Barrier, M (1999)
Hollywood Cartoons:
American Animation in the Golden Age
New York & Oxford: OUP

Beck, J (1994)
The 50 Greatest Cartoons
Atlanta: Turner Publishing Co

Bendazzi, G (1994)
Cartoons: 100 Years of Cartoon Animation
London: John Libbey

Brion, P (1990)
Tom and Jerry: The Definitive Guide to their
Animated Adventures
New York: Crown

Bruce Holman, L (1975)
Puppet Animation in the Cinema:
History and Technique
Cranberry: New Jersey

Cabarga, L (1988)
The Fleischer Story
New York: Da Capo

Crafton, D (1993)
Before Mickey:
The Animated Film 1898–1928
Chicago: University of Chicago Press

Eliot, M (1994)
Walt Disney:
Hollywood's Dark Prince
London: André Deutsch

Frierson, M (1993)
Clay Animation: American Highlights
1908–Present
New York: Twayne

Holliss, R & Sibley, B (1988)
The Disney Studio Story
New York: Crown

Kenner H (1994)
Chuck Jones:
A Flurry Of Drawings
Berkeley: University of California Press

Maltin, L (1987)
Of Mice and Magic
A History of American Animated Cartoons
New York: New American Library

Manvell, R (1980)
Art and Animation: The Story of Halas and
Batchelor Animation Studio 1940–1980
Keynsham: Clive Farrow

Merritt, R & Kaufman, JB (1993)
Walt in Wonderland:
The Silent Films of Walt Disney
Baltimore & Maryland: John Hopkins
University Press

Sandler, K (ed) (1998)
Reading the Rabbit:
Explorations in Warner Bros. Animation
New Brunswick: Rutgers University Press

Art and animation

Allan, R (1999)
Walt Disney and Europe
London: John Libbey

Faber, L & Walters, H (2004)
Animation Unlimited: Innovative Short Films Since 1940
London: Laurence King Publishing

Finch, C (1988)
The Art of Walt Disney: From Mickey Mouse to Magic Kingdoms
New York: Portland House

Gravett, P (2004)
Manga:
Sixty Years of Japanese Comics
London: Laurence King Publishing

Halas, V and Wells, P (2006)
Halas & Batchelor Cartoons:
An Animated History
London: Southbank Publishing

Jones, C (1990)
Chuck Amuck
London: Simon & Schuster

Jones, C (1996)
Chuck Reducks
New York: Time Warner

McCarthy, H (2002)
Hayao Miyazaki: Master of Japanese Animation
Berkeley, California: Stone Bridge Press

Pointon, M (ed) (1995)
Art History
[Cartoon: Caricature: Animation]
Vol 18, No 1, March 1995

Russett, R & Starr, C (1988)
Experimental Animation:
Origins of a New Art
New York: Da Capo

Wells, P (1997) (ed)
Art and Animation
London: Academy Group/
John Wiley

Wiedemann, J (ed) (2005)
Animation Now!
London & Los Angeles: Taschen

Withrow, S (2003)
Toon Art
Lewes: Ilex

Animation practice

Beckerman, H (2004)
Animation: The Whole Story
New York: Allworth Press

Birn, J (2000)
Digital Lighting and Rendering
Berkeley, Ca: New Riders Press

Blair, P (1995)
Cartoon Animation
Laguna Hills, Ca: Walter Foster Publishing

Corsaro, S & Parrott, CJ (2004)
Hollywood 2D Digital Animation
New York: Thompson Delmar Learning

Culhane, S (1988)
Animation:
From Script to Screen
London: Columbus Books

Demers, O (2001)
Digital Texturing and Painting
Berkeley, Ca: New Riders Press

Gardner, G (2001)
Gardner's Storyboard Sketchbook
Washington, New York & London: GGC Publishing

Gardner, G (2002)
Computer Graphics and Animation: History, Careers, Expert Advice
Washington, New York & London: GGC Publishing

Hooks, E (2000)
Acting for Animators
Portsmouth, NH: Heinemann

Horton, A (1998)
Laughing Out Loud
Writing the Comedy Centred Screenplay
Los Angeles: University of California Press

Johnson, O & Thomas, F (1981)
The Illusion of Life
New York: Abbeville Press

Kerlow, IV (2003)
The Art of 3D Computer Animation and Effects
New York: John Wiley & Sons

Kuperberg, M (2001)
Guide to Computer Animation
Boston & Oxford: Focal Press

Laybourne, K (1998)
The Animation Book
Three Rivers MI: Three Rivers Press

Lord, P & Sibley, B (1999)
Cracking Animation:
The Aardman Book of 3D Animation
London: Thames & Hudson

McKee, R (1999)
Story
London: Methuen

Meglin, N (2001)
Humorous Illustration
New York: Watson-Guptill Publications

Neuwirth, A (2003)
Makin' Toons:
Inside the Most Popular Animated TV
Shows & Movies
New York: Allworth Press

Patmore, C (2003)
The Complete Animation Course
London: Thames & Hudson

Pilling, J (2001)
2D and Beyond
Hove & Crans-pès-Céligny: Rotovision

Ratner, P (2003)
3-D Human Modelling and Animation
New York: John Wiley & Sons

Ratner, P (2004)
Mastering 3-D Animation
New York: Allworth Press

Roberts, S (2004)
Character Animation in 3D
Boston & Oxford: Focal Press

Scott, J (2003)
How to Write for Animation
Woodstock & New York: Overlook Press

Segar, L. (1990)
Creating Unforgettable Characters
New York: Henry Holt & Co

Shaw, S (2008)
Stop Motion:
Craft Skills for Model Animation
Boston & Oxford: Focal Press

Simon, M (2003)
Producing Independent 2D Character Animation
Boston & Oxford: Focal Press

Simon, M (2005)
Storyboards: Motion in Art
Boston & Oxford: Focal Press

Subotnick, S (2003)
Animation in the Home Digital Studio
Boston & Oxford: Focal Press

Taylor, R (1996)
The Encyclopaedia of Animation Techniques
Boston & Oxford: Focal Press

Tumminello, W (2003)
Exploring Storyboarding
Boston & Oxford: Focal Press

Webber, M (2000)
Gardner's Guide to Animation Scriptwriting
Washington, New York & London: GGC Publishing

Webber, M (2002)
Gardner's Guide to Feature Animation Writing
Washington, New York & London: GGC Publishing

Wells, P (2007)
Scriptwriting
Lausanne & Worthing: AVA Academia

Winder, C & Dowlatabadi, Z (2001)
Producing Animation
Boston & Oxford: Focal Press

The following films are referred to in this book:

2D or Not 2D (2004)
A Close Shave (1995)
Air ! (1972)
All Nothing (1979)
Animal Farm (1954)
Animated World Faiths : The Story of Guru Nanak (1998)
Azur and Asmar (2006)
Bad Luck Blackie (1949)
Balance (1950)
Bambi (1941)
Blood and Iron (2007)
Bob the Builder (1999)
Body Beautiful (1990)
Boy Who Saw The Iceberg, The (1999)
Britannia (1993)
Captain Scarlet (2005)
Cat's Cradle (1974)
Curious Cow (2000)
David (1977)
Dreams and Desires – Family Ties (2006)
Elles (1992)
End of the World in 4 Seasons (1995)
Fantasia (1940)
Father and Daughter (2000)
Father Christmas (1991)
Feet of Song (1988)
Finding Nemo (2003)
Francis (2007)
Frankenstein's Cat (2008)
Fudget's Budget (1954)
Funnybones (1995)
Grizzly Tales for Gruesome Kids (2000)
Gerald McBoing Boing (1950)
Gertie the Dinosaur (1914)
Girls Night Out (1986)
Homo Zombies (2003)
How to Kiss (1989)
Huckleberry Hound, Show, The (1958)
Humorous Phases of Funny Faces (1906)
I Move, So I Am (1997)

Idiots and Angels (2008)
Incredibles, The (2004)
Iron Giant, The (1999)
Jungle Book, The (1967)
King of the Birds (1996)
King Size Canary (1947)
Light of Uncertainty (1998)
Little Rural Riding Hood (1949)
Man Alive (1952)
Man Who Planted Trees, The (1987)
Man With a Movie Camera (1929)
Marin (2007)
Mars Attacks! (1996)
Mighty River, The (1995)
Muppet Show, The (1976)
Oktapodi (2007)
Old Man and the Sea, The (1999)
Olympia (1938)
On Land, At Sea & In the Air (1980)
One of Those Days (1988)
Pas De Deux (1968)
Pearce Sisters, The (2007)
Porco Rosso (1992)
Ratatouille (2007)
Renaissance (2006)
Rescued By Rover (1905)
Rooty Toot Toot (1951)
Rowlandson Rides Again (1999)
Ruff 'n' Reddy (1957)
Samurai Jack (2001)
Sea Song (1999)
Sir Gawain and the Green Knight (2002)
Sita Sings the Blues (2008)
Snow White and the Seven Dwarfs (1937)
Snowman, The (1982)
Soma (2001)
South Park (1997)
Spirited Away (2001)
Star Wars (1977)
Steamboat Willie (1928)
Sunny Side Up (1985)
Superglue (1987)
Sword of Storms (2006)
Tea at Number Ten (1987)

Terkel in Trouble (2004)
Triangle (1994)
Triumph of the Will (1935)
Uncles and Aunts (1989)
Waterpeople (1995)
What Might Be (2006)
When the Wind Blows (1986)
Wife of Bath, The (1998)
Yellow Submarine (1968)

The following are also useful to watch for their approaches to drawing:

6 Weeks in June (1998)
Across the Fields (1992)
All the Drawings of the Town (1959)
Allegro Non Tropo (1976)
At the End of the Earth (1999)
Big Snit, The (1985)
Bird in the Window (1996)
Birds, Bees and Storks (1964)
Breakfast on the Grass (1987)
Cat Came Back, The (1998)
Chicken Sandwich (2001)
Christopher Crumpet (1953)
Doubled Up (2004)
Drawn from Memory (1995)
Franz Kafka (1999)
Intolerance I, II, III (2000–2003)
Island of Black Mor, The (2004)
JoJo in the Stars (2003)
Man With the Beautiful Eyes, The (1999)
Media (1999)
Mt Head (2002)
Passing Days (1969)
Pleasures of War (1998)
Repete (1995)
Ring of Fire (2000)
Satiemania (1978)
Sisyphus (1967)
Sobriety, Obesity and Growing Old (1991)
TRANSIT (1997)
Trouble Indemnity (1950)
Who I Am and What I Want (2005)

www.karmatoons.com
Doug Compton's personal site is very helpful for
those creating classical animated drawing.

www.animationmentor.com
This is a comprehensive (if expensive) site for
committed animators wishing to animate to a
professional standard, which prioritises
approaches to classical animation for
digital applications.

www.awn.com
Animation World Network – simply the key
resource for the animation community worldwide,
including articles, information and news.

www.johnkstuff.blogspot.com
John Kricfalusi's blogspot recommending
particular analyses of cartoons and relevant
publications about 'golden era' animation.

www.cooltoons2.com
Information about television cartoons.

www.microsoft.com
Advice and support about producing online
animation, appropriating ideas from traditional
animation processes.

www.cartoonbrew.com
News and commentary on the animation industry
from CartoonResearch.com's Jerry Beck and
AnimationBlast.com's Amid Amidi, both
established authors on American cartoon history.

www.animationacademy.co.uk
Website for the Animation Academy at
Loughborough University, creators of the
Animation Workshop initiative.

P3 Courtesy Richard Reeves

P7 Courtesy The Halas and Batchelor Collection Limited

P8 'Felix the Cat' courtesy Library of Congress

P9 Betty Boop Model Sheet – Fleischer Bros. Courtesy Library of Congress

P10 Man Alive! Courtesy Tee Bosustow

P20; 129 'Charmin' advertisement images courtesy Procter & Gamble

P23 Courtesy Ward Kimball

P24 The Third Class Carriage, c.1862–64 (oil on canvas) (b/w photo), Daumier, Honoré (1808–79) / Metropolitan Museum of Art, New York, USA / The Bridgeman Art Library

P25 La Clowness Looks Around, Mademoiselle Cha-U-Kao (lithograph) by Toulouse-Lautrec, Henri de (1864–1901) Queensland Art Gallery, Brisbane, Australia / The Bridgeman Art Library: Seated Dancer, c.1881–83 (pastel on paper) by Degas, Edgar (1834–1917). Musée d'Orsay, Paris, France / Giraudon / The Bridgeman Art Library

P27 Study of Arms (pen & ink on paper), Vinci, Leonardo da (1452–1519) (attr. to) / Louvre, Paris, France / Giraudon / The Bridgeman Art Library

P39 'John Bull's Progress', pub. by Hannah Humphrey, 1793 (etching) (b&w photo), Gillray, James (1757–1815) / British Museum, London, UK / The Bridgeman Art Library

P46; 74 'Whiskas' advertisement images Courtesy Mars, Incorporated. All Rights Reserved. ®/TM Whiskas, Trademark of Mars, Incorporated and its affiliates

P48; 50; 54; 55; 60–65; 102–105 Courtesy Peter Parr

P55; 71; 100 Courtesy Kimberley Rice

P66–67 Courtesy Animation Workshop

P72 Courtesy Michel Ocelot

P77 Courtesy Michael Shaw

P82–83 Courtesy Clive Walley

P85 Shira Avni

P86–89 Courtesy Right Angle Productions

P91–92 Courtesy A. Film

P93–95 Courtesy Marmier et al.

P96–99 Courtesy Michel Ocelot

P112–115 Courtesy Alexandre Bernard, Pierre Pages and Damien Laurent

P116–117 Courtesy Erica Russell

P118–123 Courtesy Curtis Jobling

P124–127 Courtesy Al Hirschfeld and JJ Sedelmaier

P126–127 Courtesy JJ Sedelmaier

P130–133 Courtesy Tim Fernée

P134–139 Courtesy Let Me Feel Your Finger First

P141 Hellboy Animated: Sword of Storms. Courtesy Dark Horse Publications LLP

P141–147 Courtesy Nina Paley

P148; 154–157 Courtesy Paul Driessen

P150–151 Storyboards for The Man Who Planted Trees courtesy Frédéric Back © Atelier Frédéric Back inc.

P153 Still from The Man Who Planted Trees courtesy Radio-Canada-CBC

P158–161 Courtesy Richard Reeves

P162–165 Michael Dudok de Wit

P167–168; 170–171 Stills from The Pearce Sisters by Luis Cook © Aardman Animation Ltd. 2007

P172; 174–6 Courtesy Gerrit van Dijk

P180–181 Courtesy Tim Fernée

P182–183 Courtesy Bill Plympton

P184–185 Courtesy Deanna Marsigliese

All reasonable attempts have been made to clear permissions and trace and credit the copyright holders of the images reproduced in this book. However, if any credits have been inadvertently omitted, the publisher will endeavour to incorporate amendments in future editions.

Many thanks to Tamasin Cole for the design of this book and to Caroline Walmsley, Georgia Kennedy, Brian Morris and Renée Last for once again keeping the show on the road and helping me through some tough moments…

Others in need of great thanks:
Mette Peters
Brian Wells
Eric Serre
Marie Foulston
Helen Neno
Dave Burgess
Chris Hinton
Steve Bell
William Kentridge
Marie Christine Demers
Kerry Drumm
Shelley Page
Magali Montet
Rebecca Battle
Peter Chung

And, of course, all the named artists and scholars throughout the text.